ROBINSON CR~~~

A PANTOMIME

JIM SPERINCK

Jasper Publishing

1 Broad St Hemel Hempstead Herts HP2 5BW
Tel; 01442 63461 Fax; 01442 217102

Jasper Publishing

1 Broad Street   Hemel Hempstead
Herts   HP2 5BW
Tel; 01442 63461 Fax; 01442 217102

ISBN 1 874009 45 7

iii

CHARACTERS

Baroness Bossalot	snobbish mother of Rosie
Rosie	in love with Robinson Crusoe
Robinson Crusoe	
Mrs Crusoe	his mother
Cedric	friend of Rosie and Robinson
Captain Hook, Long John Silver, Morgan, Blackbeard	a pirate
Mr Mate	his Mate
Queen Neptune	
King Rumble Tum/Bert Crusoe	Robinson's long lost father
Man (United) Friday	Island friend of Robinson
Warrior 1	
Warrior 2	
Olly the Octopus	

General Chorus as: Townsfolk, sailors, pirates, sea creatures, island natives, warriors, Neptune's assistants etc.,

SYNOPSIS OF SCENES

ACT 1

Scene 1	Plymouth Harbour
Scene 2	A street in Plymouth
Scene 3	On board the Jolly Roger
Scene 4	On the Sea Bed
Scene 5	King Neptune's Throne Room

ACT 2

Scene 1	Robinson Crusoe's Island Camp
Scene 2	A Deserted Beach
Scene 3	King Rumble Tum's Camp
Scene 4	Mrs Crusoe's Waiting Room
Scene 5	A Castle in Plymouth

Scenery may be kept very simple if desired. Alternatively, this pantomime offers the opportunity to put on a really lavish production - the choice is yours. There is a short, interact scene, between each of the main scenes that will allow sufficient time for big scene changes. These interact scenes can easily be played in front of tabs, or, if facilities allow, a front cloth.

Most principals can wear the same costume throughout the show, with the possible exception of the finale scene. Please refer to the Production Notes at the end of the script.

NOTES ON THE CHARACTERS

Baroness Bossalot. A thorough snob. She wants her daughter to marry the rich Cedric, and not her chosen Robinson. Can double with Queen Neptune, if desired. Female.

Rosie. Principal girl. A straight, demanding role. She is determined to marry Robinson, in spite of her mother's wishes. Female.

Robinson Crusoe. Principal boy. A fairly straight and demanding part. Full of good principles, upright and honourable. Female.

Mrs Crusoe. A traditional Dame. An eccentric character, energetic, full of life, who enjoys her own jokes immensely, Must be able to dominate, change mood quickly, and interact with the audience. Male.

Cedric. Young comedy part. Upper class, but loyal, friend of Rosie and Robinson. Male, but could be female.

Captain Hook, Long John Silver, Morgan, Blackbeard. A completely "over the top" eccentric character. A dishonest, lovable rogue, who talks to his parrot all the time, and answers back in a comic attempt at ventriloquism. A very demanding character part, which will call for considerable confidence, experience, and stage presence. Male.

Mate. Side-kick, and foil, to the Captain. A simple-hearted fellow who should have the audience on his side, as he bears the brunt of the Captain's humour, and tells his child-like jokes. Male, but could be female.

King Rumble Tum. Dreaded ruler of Robinson's Desert Island. It is best not to disclose (in programme etc.,) his true identity, and retain the element of surprise. A small part, but must be able to completely change character. Male.

Man (United) Friday. A supporting role. Football crazy, superstitious, Desert Island friend of Robinson. Male.

Queen Neptune. Long-suffering wife of Neptune. Combining the qualities of a queen, with those of a tour guide! She decides to assist Robinson and Rosie, and to thwart the greedy Baroness Bossalot, with whom she can double, if desired. Female.

Warriors. King Rumble Tum's guards. The lines can be spoken by one, or shared out between two, or more. Male.

Olly the Octopus. Lovable pet of Queen Neptune. Male or female junior member of the cast.

MUSICAL NUMBERS

The songs included here are suggestions only for the type of music that can be used. Final choice is left to the Musical Director.

Please note that permission from **Jasper Publishing** to perform this play **does** **not** include permission to use copyright songs and music suggested here. Performers are urged to consult the **Performing Right Society** (see note below).

Overture - Theme music, West Country folk songs, songs of the sea etc.,

1.	Opening number, "The Best Of Times Is Now" or "Fortuosity" or another	Full chorus
2.	Duet, "Somewhere, There's A Place For Us" or "Beyond The Blue Horizon" or "To Dream The Impossible Dream"	Rosie and Robinson
3.	"I Am A Pirate King" or another	Captain and Mate
4.	"We've Got To Leave Our Plymouth Hoe" (We've Got To Leave Old Durham Town, adapted) or another	Mrs Crusoe, Rosie, Cedric, and Robinson
5.	"All The Nice Girls Love A Sailor" or "We Sail The Ocean Blue"	Full chorus
6.	"When The Foeman Bears His Steel"	Full chorus
7.	Dance of the Sea Creatures, "The Onedin Line" or "The Octopus's Garden" or "La Mer"	Junior chorus
8.	House song, "If You Go Down To The Sea Today" or "Tiptoe Through The Seaweed" or "Three Little Fishes"	Rosie, the Sea Creatures, and Robinson
9.	"We're Having A Heat Wave" or "Oh Island In The Sun"	Full chorus

10.	"An Old-Fashioned Millionaire" or Diamonds Are A Girl's Best Friend"	Mrs Crusoe
11.	"Whatever We Do, Wherever We Go" or another	Cedric, Rosie, Robinson and Man Friday
12.	"Money, Money, Money" or "Money Makes The World Go Around"	Rosie, Robinson Mrs Crusoe, Man Friday and Cedric
13.	Warrior Dance	Full Chorus
14.	"Everything's Coming Up Roses" or "Look For The Silver Lining" or "On A Wonderful Day Like Today"	Full chorus
15.	"Say Robinson Crusoe" (Gee Officer Krupke, West Side Story) or another	Full chorus

*The following statement (provided by the **Performing Right Society Ltd.,**) concerning the use of music, is included here for your attention.*

The permission of the owner of the performing right in copyright music must be obtained before any public performance may be given, whether in conjunction with a play or sketch or otherwise, and this permission is just as necessary for amateur performances as for professional. The majority of copyright musical works (other than oratorios, musical plays and similar dramatico-musical works) are controlled in the British Commonwealth by the **Performing Right Society Ltd., 29-33 Berners Street, London W1P 4AA.**

The Society's practice is to issue licences authorising the use of its repertoire to the proprietors of premises at which music is publicly performed, or, alternatively, to the organisers of musical entertainment, but the Society does not require payment of fees by performers as such. Producers or promoters of plays, sketches etc., at which music is to be performed, during or after the play or sketch, should ascertain whether the premises at which the performances are to be given are covered by a licence issued by the Society, and if they are not, should make application to the Society for particulars as to the fee payable.

Also available in this series
by **Jim Sperinck**

ROBINSON CRUSOE

ACT 1

After the overture, to a dramatic chord, the curtains open

Scene 1

Plymouth Harbour. Backcloth should show a Georgian harbour scene, with a timbered Inne on one side, and a warehouse, or whatever, on the other. The masts of sailing ships should be visible, the foremost being the vessel of Captain Long John Silver, Hook, Morgan, Blackbeard. There should be an entrance from both wings, plus, if possible, a separate entrance from the Inne. On stage should be various harbour paraphernalia; barrels, boxes, capstans etc.,

As the curtains open there are a full chorus of; sailors, townsfolk, street-urchins, pick-pockets, merchants, street-traders etc., all going about their business. When the scene has established itself they sing the opening number

Song No 1

'The Best of Times is Now' or 'Fortuosity' or 'It's a Hap, Hap, Happy Day' A lively dance routine should accompany the song

At the end of the song, some chorus wander off, others continue with work, and Mrs Crusoe and Robinson enter

Mrs Crusoe But she can't do that, the miserable old bat! (*notices audience*) Ooh look, there's some people out there. I wonder what they've come for? (*to audience*) No, the Social Security's further down!
Robinson Mother! That's the audience!
Mrs Crusoe 'Course it is. D'you think I didn't know that? I'm not daft!
Robinson (*with exaggerated innocence*) Of course not mother.
Mrs Crusoe Now, say hello to the nice people Robinson.
Robinson Hello.
Mrs Crusoe (*to audience*) Say hello to Robinson.
Audience Hello.
Mrs Crusoe (*to Robinson*) That's not very loud, is it? I think they can do better than that, don't you?

Robinson Ask them again. They're not warmed up yet.

Mrs Crusoe Not warmed up? (*to audience, very bossy*) Get yourselves warmed up then. Jump about a bit if you like. Do some aerobics in the aisle, we won't mind. Now, can you say it louder? Really shout this time. HELLO ROBINSON!

Audience HELLO ROBINSON!

Mrs Crusoe That's better. This is my son, Robinson you see, and I'm Mrs Crusoe. We've just had a bit of bad news.

Robinson (*encouraging the audience to 'Ah'*) AH!

Mrs Crusoe Oh no. It's worse than that. A bit of <u>very</u> bad news.

Robinson (*encouraging the audience to 'Ah' louder*) AH!

Mrs Crusoe A bit of <u>very very</u> bad news.

Robinson (*pulling a face, and encouraging an even louder 'Ah'*) AH!

Mrs Crusoe Yes that's about how bad it was. Now, what was that bit of bad news we had?

Robinson About Baroness Bossalot mother.

Mrs Crusoe I remember! It was about Baroness Bossy-bloomers. (*indicating audience*) Tell them about her?

Robinson It won't make any difference, she's made up her mind.

Mrs Crusoe Robinson, if you don't tell them soon, they'll start going home.

Robinson Alright mother. It's the Baroness you see...

Mrs Crusoe (*pushing him out of the way*) The lady that owns the house where we live. She's chucking us out.

Robinson Yes, she's throwing us out and...

Mrs Crusoe (*pushing him again*) Just because we're a bit behind with the rent. What a cheek! I'd push her face in, but I think someone's already done it!

Robinson Yes and...

Mrs Crusoe Do you mind? I'm telling them.

Robinson But you said...

Mrs Crusoe That's not the real reason though. Oh no!

Robinson Mother! Don't!

Mrs Crusoe Don't talk when I'm interrupting dear. It's rude. No. She's got a very different reason. I know what she's up to. Shall I tell you the real reason?

Audience Yes.

Mrs Crusoe It's because her daughter Rosie is sweet on my Robinson. Yes, that's why. She thinks we're not good enough for her! The rotten old cabbage leaf! Just because she owns half the town! Oow, just you let me get at her. I'll do her a mischief I will! (*rolls her sleeves up and begins to pace up and down*)

Robinson (*trying to restrain her*) Mother! Calm down. You'll bring on your old problem if you go on like this.

Mrs Crusoe Problem? I'll give <u>her</u> problem. All fur coat and no...

Robinson MOTHER!

Mrs Crusoe Oh I wish your father was here to defend us.

Robinson But he's been gone for ages.

Mrs Crusoe Gone! I'll give him 'gone' when he gets back. (*to audience*) I sent him out for a packet of frozen peas, seven - no eight years ago, and he hasn't been seen since. Oh it's no use Robinson! We must give up hope.

Robinson Don't say that mother.

Mrs Crusoe Well of course it is. They'll be all thawed out by now! I can't understand it. He always came home when he wanted something a bit special - you know - when he got hungry. If they bring him back alive, I'll murder him!

House lights up as she goes down into the audience

Oh you can't trust men, can you? (*picks lady member of the audience*) You know that don't you? Course you do. You can tell she knows. (*she begins to search for him in the audience*) I'll just check and see if he's out here. They say that crimin-imin-inimals always return to the scene of the crime, don't they? Can anyone see him out here? He'll be the one with the frozen peas. (*selects another lady member of the audience*) You haven't seen him have you? I don't think she'd give him back if she had. (*to a man*) Ooh, this one looks alright! Is he spoken for? Yes? Pity!

She returns to the stage. House lights down

It's no use. I'd never get used to a new one. Well you get to know their little ways, don't you? You know - like - where they leave their dirty socks Have you noticed, you can only ever find one, can't you? I wonder what they do with the other one? Still my husband was very hygienic. Oh yes. He always put on a clean pair of socks every morning. And by the end of the week he couldn't get his shoes on! Oh! The old jokes are best!

Enter Rosie

Rosie Hello Robinson. Hello Mrs Crusoe.

Robinson Hello Rosie.

Mrs Crusoe Huh! We're not talking to anyone in your family.

Robinson Mother! It's not Rosie's fault.

Rosie Thank you Robinson. I'm sorry about mother, Mrs Crusoe. I tried to talk her out of it. I said, 'If you throw them out, I'm going too'.

Mrs Crusoe Going to what?

Rosie Going as well.

Robinson Rosie, let's go to sea and find some deserted island where we can be together for always.

Mrs Crusoe Oh Gawd! Youth! I can see what they're leading up to - a song. I'm going home to pack. *(to Robinson)* Just one quick verse and home you - there's work to do. *(exits)*

Robinson *(calling after her)* Yes mother.

Rosie Are you serious Robinson - about finding a desert island, and us being together for always?

Robinson Of course Rosie.

Song No 2

A duet from Rosie and Robinson. 'Somewhere - There's a Place for Us' or 'Beyond the Blue Horizon' or 'To Dream the Impossible Dream' or another

At the end of the song, enter Baroness Bossalot

Bossalot What's going on here? What are you doing speaking to this common person? I gave you strict instructions Rosie.

Robinson Baroness Bossalot, Rosie and I want to get married.

Bossalot Huh! You might want to, but you're certainly not going to. Rosie is going to marry Cedric.

Rosie I'm not going to marry Cedric. Cedric's soppy.

Bossalot Soppy Cedric's soppy! Soppy Cedric's not soppy! And what if he is? His father's rich, and that's what matters!

Rosie Oh no it isn't!

Bossalot Oh yes it is.

Robinson encourages the audience to join in

Rosie Oh no it isn't.

Bossalot *(to audience)* Oh yes it is.

Audience Oh no it isn't!

Bossalot Will you be quiet out there, you rabble?

Audience No!

Bossalot It's nothing to do with you. No it isn't.

Audience Yes it is!

Bossalot If you lived in Plymouth, I'd have you thrown out as well. Yes I would!

Audience No you wouldn't!

Bossalot I don't know what the world's coming to. I don't. They'll be giving you the vote next. I'll get Mr Major *(or whoever)* to sort you out. Yes I will.

Audience No you won't!

Bossalot Now I brought Cedric with me. Where's he got to? Cedric!

Enter Cedric backwards, looking around, he sees the audience and jumps

Cedric Oh, I say! Hello Robinson. It's jolly nice here, old chap, isn't it?

Robinson Hello Cedric.

Bossalot *(to Robinson)* Shouldn't you be helping your mother to pack?

Robinson Oh dear! I'd forgotten. I'll be back soon Rosie. *(exits)*

Bossalot Oh don't hurry, please. *(to audience)* There! Don't they look a lovely couple? I'll leave you two to have a nice chat. I'm sure you've got some important arrangements to make! Like where we're all going to live when you're married, and all that lovely money is in one family - my family! *(exits)*

Rosie Oh Cedric! You're very sweet, but, you know I could only marry Robinson?

Cedric I know that Rosie, old girl. Don't trouble yourself on my account. I only wish I could jolly well help, don't you know. Your mother, well, she has a very determined bent at times.

Rosie You mean all the time Cedric.

Cedric We could all go to sea to escape from her.

Rosie That's funny!

Cedric *(puzzled)* Oh! Is it?

Rosie Yes, Robinson said the same thing just now.

Cedric Oh. It's a very big decision old girl. You're not thinking of taking your mother with you, are you?

Rosie Of course not.

Cedric Alright then, I'll come as well.

Rosie Good. Let's go and find Robinson.

Both exit. Enter Captain, unsteadily, from the Inne, with his Mate

Captain Ah! That be a good drop o' beer that be. Ow aah! Ain't that right Polly! Now me old shipmate. Have we got a crew for the voyage?

Mate Not yet Captain.

Captain What! No crew! That's very serious that is.

Mate The men didn't like the way you kept flogging 'em boss.

Captain Flogging 'em? What d'you mean?

Mate Well. You flogged the First Mate to that Dutch Captain for a fiver. Then flogged the Cook to that Chinese Junk for a takeaway. Then you flogged the...

Captain Yes, alright. Don't go on. We had a cash flow problem, didn't we?

Mate Yes. The cash turned into rum and flowed down your throat.

Captain Er. I should 'a flogged you.

Mate You tried hard enough, but nobody wanted to buy me.

Captain Huh! I wonder why!

Mate I can't find anyone who wants to sail with us boss.

Captain I can't sail wi'out a crew Matey. What do you think I pays you for?

Mate Sorry boss.

Captain Did you try bribin' 'em?

Mate Yes. They said they'd seen that chocolate money before.

Captain Did you try tellin' em lies?

Mate Yes. I told them all about how they was bound to find hidden treasure, and beautiful dancing girls on despotic beaches.

Captain Despotic beaches! You mean exotic beaches!

Mate Yes that's right carbolic beaches.

Captain Well? Surely the idea of beautiful maidens, and treasure on carbolic beaches tempted 'em?

Mate No. They said they'd been to Blackpool (*or local town*) already.

Captain Mangle me mizzenmast! What's wrong with people round here? Ain't they got no spirit of adventure? My Grandfather fought with Francis Drake. He fought with Walter Raleigh too.

Mate Yes. Your Grandfather couldn't get on with nobody.

Captain Tis true! Tis true! Ha, ha! Did you try hitting 'em over the head?

Mate Yes boss.

Captain Well! What happened?

Mate They hit me back. I've still got a big bump on me head just here, look. (*he tries to show the Captain, who is not interested*) It don't half hurt. Can you put some plaster on it for me?

Captain Shiver me timbers! You'll 'ave a big bump somewheres if I starts on you. What we going to do eh Polly? Who's a pretty boy then? (*does bad ventriloquist act, trying to mask his mouth*) You are. You are. Ahaa. Ha, ha!

Mate Here boss. I was wondering. How do you catch parrots?

Captain It's easy Matey. You 'ang upside down from a tree, and make a noise like a nut! Ha, ha! What d'you think o' that one, eh Polly?

Enter Rosie, Cedric and Robinson, who stay together on one side of the stage

Hey up! What about this lot then? They look like an able-bodied crew.

Captain and Mate, on the other side of the stage, listen to the conversation

Rosie So, shall we go then?

Robinson Maybe we'll get rich. Find some treasure.

Captain Hear that? They're after some treasure.

Captain and Mate edge nearer

Robinson If we were rich your mother would have to agree to our marriage.

Cedric You can have some of my money, old boy. I've got more than I need. How about some of my British Telecom shares?

Robinson That's kind of you Cedric, but we've got to find money of our own.

Rosie It would be nice to find buried treasure and be independent of mother.

Captain There it is again. That magic word. Treasure! They know where there's some treasure buried. Come on Matey. *(approaching Robinson's group)* Heave to me hearties. Fancy a nice trip round the bay then?

Robinson Who are you?

Cedric They look like scoundrels to me, Robinson. See if you've lost your wallet.

Captain I'm Captain Morgan, Long John Silver, Blackbeard, Hook, an honest seafaring man, your reverence. Ha, ha! Who's a pretty boy then? Who's a pretty boy? You are! You are! Ha, ha!

Rosie That's a mouthful of a name.

Captain Ow ah! Ow ah! Me mother knew a lot of sailors you see. Very friendly type she was. Didn't know which one to name me after, so she named me after them all! Ha, ha! Who's a pretty... Oh shut your face! That's my ship there.

Mate Yes, the Jolly Roger.

Captain *(kicking the Mate)* Shut up you fool! Dodger, The Jolly Dodger he means. He rolls his 'R's funny.

They all try to look behind him. The Mate, embarrassed, tries to cover himself

Captain Yes. The Jolly Dodger, your eminence, on account of it dodges the waves you see. Specially designed. Yes. That's it. Ain't that right Polly?

Mate I didn't know that boss.

Captain What, you didn't know she were specially designed?

Mate No, I didn't know I rolled my 'R's funny.

Cedric Don't trust him, Robinson. Looks like rotten Stilton to me.

Captain Take no notice of Matey here, your worship. No. He's one cannon short of a broadside see. Yes, he's a bit dyslex... dyslex... Gawd! I think I am as well! What I means is, insanity runs in his family. It certainly didn't have to run very fast to catch him anyroads! Ha, ha! What d'you think o' that one, eh Polly?

Mate What's insanity boss?

Captain Insanity? It's when you don't wash your socks and your drains smell all horrible, ain't it. Ha, ha!

Mate *(looking round, puzzled)* Oh. Where's me drains then boss? *(now commences to sniff under his arms, and to try to smell his feet etc.,)*

They all watch Mate

Captain (*confidentially*) Don't mind him. Dropped on his head you see.
Rosie Ah, at an early age?
Captain No, in a minute, if he don't pack it in!
Cedric (*to the Captain*) I say old boy. Why has your parrot got such short legs?
Captain Cos, if his legs was longer, the eggs would 'ave further to fall, and they'd break when they landed you see!
Cedric Oh, really!
Mate Boss, do you know where to take Polly if she needs spectacles?
Captain I don't know!
Mate To the Birds-Eye shop! He, he.
Captain Oh very droll. But this 'ere is a very intelligent parrot, your worships.
Cedric Is it?
Captain Oh yes. You see, if you pull his left leg, he sings, 'Land of 'ope and Glory'. And, if you pull 'is other leg, he sings, 'The Fishermen of England'.
Mate And what does he do if you pull both his legs?
Captain He falls flat on 'is back, you fool!
Robinson That's enough parrot jokes for now. I'm sure there'll be more later.
Cedric Oh no there won't.
Captain Oh yes there will!
Robinson Look, can you take us on your next trip then?
Captain Well, let me see now. that won't be easy.
Mate But boss, you said...

A crash as he receives another kick from the Captain

Captain There's a lot of work to do on a ship you see.
Robinson We could work.
Captain Could you now? Well, in return for a little work... I could perhaps... take a chance. Ah, me generous nature, it'll be me undoing. Eh, Polly?
Cedric Just a minute. Where are you bound for, my good man?
Captain Oh all over the seven seas, your benevolence. Yes. If it's wet, it's me home. Ain't that right Polly eh?
Cedric Fella's cracked, if you ask me. Talking to a bally budgie all the time.
Captain (*in a stage whisper to the Mate*) Just you wait 'til I gets that soppy one on board. I'll knock a few sparks off him. I'll give him, `La di da, La di da'.
Cedric What was that?
Captain I said, 'Ow ah, ow ah, ha, ha'.
Cedric He's fallen out of his crow's-nest, on his bonce, Robinson.
Robinson We must do something Cedric. This is a desperate situation.

Cedric Well alright. But I insist on coming too. Strength in numbers old boy.

Captain Is it a bargain then?

Robinson Rosie, is it agreed?

Rosie Yes, it's agreed.

Robinson It's a bargain then.

They all shake hands

Robinson Let's collect what we need for the journey. And don't let your mother know what you're doing.

Rosie Of course not.

They exit, leaving Captain and Mate on stage

Captain There's our crew then. All sorted. I'm a genius. Who's a clever boy then? Who's a clever boy? You are! You are!

Mate What's a genius boss?

Captain It's when you give all your money away, ain't it!

Mate That can't be you then. Anyway that's generous boss.

Captain Don't mention it lad. Ha, ha!

Mate Boss, d'you know why the Captain couldn't write in his logbook?

Captain I dunno. Why couldn't the Captain write in his logbook?

Mate Because all his hands were on deck!

Captain At thirty five, it's time you stopped reading them comics.

Mate Anyway what was all that about treasure?

Captain They know where there's some treasure hidden. I heard 'em talking about it. They've probably got a map hidden about their person...

Mate Oh! Which person's that then boss?

Captain Blister me barnacles! They're going to make their fortune. And when they've made their fortune, we're going to make our fortune by nicking their fortune. Ha, ha!

Mate Ah, but what if they nick back their fortune, which was their fortune, then our fortune, and then their fortune again, they'll have made their fortune, and we'll have no fortune.

Captain Streuth! Did you work that out all by yourself? Beam me up Spotty!

Song No 3

A solo from the Captain, with the Mate as chorus. 'I am a Pirate King' or 'You've Got to Pick a Pocket or Two' or another

At the end of the song

Captain Come on Matey. To the ship.

They make to exit, as the curtains slowly close

Scene 2

*This is an interact scene that will allow for the changing of scenery, and can be performed in front of tabs, or a frontcloth showing another part of the town. If more time is required, then **Song No 3** can be sung in front of tabs, and the curtains closed as the Captain and Mate move forward to commence their song*

Enter Mrs Crusoe, Robinson, Rosie and Cedric. Mrs Crusoe is cluttered up with all manner of odd luggage, so that she looks as comical as possible

Mrs Crusoe Where did you say we were going?

Robinson We're going to sea.

Mrs Crusoe Going to see what?

Cedric Going to sea, on the jolly old nautical what's it, don't you know.

Mrs Crusoe What on the wet water? On a real boat? How exciting it will be!

Rosie Yes it will be exciting for you.

Mrs Crusoe No! No! I mean how exciting it will be for all those big strong sailors, to have me on board.

Robinson If you say so mother.

Mrs Crusoe Oh I should have packed my water-wings.

Robinson I think you've got enough there.

Mrs Crusoe I must sit down and get on with this sock. You'll need warm socks on the boat. (*she sits on her luggage and gets out a sock that she is knitting*)

Robinson Now we must all be careful, and stick together.

Cedric And keep an eye on that Captain chappie. The one with the penguin what's it on his shoulder. He looks like a piece of mouldy Cheddar to me.

Rosie Well Robinson, this is it.

Robinson Yes. Goodbye Plymouth Hoe.

Cedric Goodbye Plymouth, old girl.

Rosie Goodbye Plymouth Hoe.

Song No 4

Quartet from Cedric, Robinson, Rosie and Mrs Crusoe. 'We've got to Leave our Plymouth Hoe' to the tune of 'I've got to leave Old Durham Town' or another

Suggested words. All sing

> We've got to leave our Plymouth Hoe.
> We've got to leave, we've got to go.
> We've got to leave our Plymouth Hoe.
> Cos old Bossalot is throwing us out.

Cedric and Mrs Crusoe sing, yawning, not enthusiastic about the idea

> We'll find an island in the sun.
> Banana cutlets sound like fun!
> Count the palm trees, one by one!
> Goodbye, we're leaving.
> Leaving, leaving, leaving, leaving, leaving.

All sing   We've got to leave our Plymouth Hoe.
> We've got to leave, we've got to go.
> We've got to leave our Plymouth Hoe.
> Cos old Bossalot is throwing us out.

Mrs Crusoe finds a handkerchief, sobs, and is assisted off stage, with her luggage by Cedric. They take up positions, centre stage, behind the curtain, facing down stage, ready for when the curtains open

Robinson   Maybe one day we'll be rich.
and Rosie   Come back home without a hitch.
> Then get married you and I.
> Till then we're leaving.
> Leaving, leaving, leaving, leaving, leaving.

> We've got to leave our Plymouth Hoe.
> We've got to leave, we've got to go.
> We've got to leave our Plymouth Hoe.
> Cos old Bossalot is throwing us out.

At the end of the song, as the curtains open, they turn and make a group with Cedric and Mrs Crusoe, looking as though they have all just arrived on board

Scene 3

*On board the Jolly Roger. The top deck of the ship, complete with rigging, sails,
flags, barrels, cases etc.,*

*As the curtains open the Captain is towards the back of the ship, on a raised
platform or case, holding a gun, looking down on Mate, and the chorus, who
are dressed as sailors and pirates, and busy preparing for the departure*

Cedric, Robinson, Rosie, and Mrs Crusoe now turn round and face the audience

Captain Set too there, land-lubbers. I pays you to work, not fall asleep. Mate!
Mate Yes Captain?
Captain Give 'em a taste of the cat o' nine tails, if they don't look lively! Ha, ha!
That's the way to do it, eh Polly?
Mate Aye, aye Captain.
Captain *(noticing Mrs Crusoe, and coming down towards her)* 'ere, what's she
doing on board? We got enough ballast. Throw her over the bulwarks.
Mrs Crusoe How dare you! I'm not going anywhere near them!
Rosie She's with us. She's got to come. She's got nowhere to live you see.
Mrs Crusoe *(abandons her luggage and paces up and down the stage in a
frenzy)* Oh! I'm homeless! Thrown out! Cast out on the streets with nowhere
to lay me head! Oh dear! What's to become of me? Where will it all end?
Captain It'll end when you're thrown over the bulwarks!
Mrs Crusoe Stop saying that! *(up and down again)* How cruel life is! A poor
helpless woman with no-one to defend me! Adrift on the raging sea of life.
Captain Gawd! She'll turn the ship's rum ration sour!
Mrs Crusoe *(off again)* Nobody cares! You work hard all your life and this is
what happens! I think I'll shoot myself!
Captain *(holding out the gun)* Here's a gun.
Mrs Crusoe *(up and down again)* If only my poor long-lost husband was here to
defend me!
Captain I can see why he left! Ha, ha!
Mrs Crusoe If only I hadn't sent him for frozen peas! It's a judgement on me!
Captain Gawd! I hate being up-staged like this! Madam, in recognition for
your many years of service to acting... *(points a gun at her and fires it with a
loud bang)*
Mrs Crusoe *(made worse by the shot)* Oh! Oh! I've been shot! Cut down in me
prime! *(feeling all over for where the wound is)* Help! Robinson, I think I've
had a nervous breakdown!
Captain I'm not surprised, after all that over-acting! Ha, ha!

Robinson Calm down mother. Don't throw a fit.

Captain Another fit you mean!

Rosie Please take her. We can't leave her behind.

Captain Leave her <u>behind</u>? We're goin' to leave <u>all</u> of 'er! Ha, ha!

Mrs Crusoe How dare you!

Robinson We all go, or we all stay. That's the deal Captain.

Rosie Well done Robinson. You tell him.

Captain But she'll be no use. What can she do, besides overact?

Mrs Crusoe Oh I come from a very nautical family, your admiralty. Why many's the time, many's the time I've polished up the Captain's binnacle! Oh yes! You just watch me - scrubbing up the quarter-deck, scrubbing up the eight bells, scrubbing the mainbrace...

Mate Right little scrubber, ain't she?

Robinson She's a good cook.

Mrs Crusoe Oh yes. You just wait 'til you see my dumplings!

Captain A cook eh! Well that's different. We could do with some home cooking.

Mrs Crusoe Just you leave everything to me. You won't believe what I can do with a ship's biscuit, your steamship!

Captain Right, that settles it. All aboard! All aboard!

Mate All aboard! All aboard!

Captain We sail with the tide! We sail with the tide!

Mate Your trousers are fried! Your trousers are fried!

Captain Cast off amidships! Cast off amidships!

Mate Cut up your giblets! Cut up your giblets!

Captain Run up the riggers.

Mate Pull up your knick....

Mrs Crusoe (*sloshing the Mate*) Do you mind! (*exits with her luggage*)

Captain Shoot the Mate!

Mate Shoot the Mate... Oh! Sorry Captain.

Captain Did you weigh the anchor?

Mate Yes Captain. Ooh, and it ain't half heavy!

Captain Shiver me timbers! 'ere we go!

As they move away from the harbour, it will be effective, if it is possible, for some piece of background stage furniture, a pole or flagpost, or a large buoy etc., to be pulled off stage slowly, on runners, behind the ship

Song No 5

Full chorus number, led by the principals, with an appropriate dance routine, 'All the Nice Girls Love a Sailor' or 'We Sail the Ocean Blue' or another

At the end of the song, most of the crew go off stage. Those who remain will be scrubbing the decks, or attending to rigging etc., The Captain remains on stage

Enter Mrs Crusoe, dressed in a ridiculous old-fashioned, Victorian type, striped bathing costume, with a large towel. The Captain watches her in disbelief

Captain Rattle me rudder! Have you ever seen anything like it eh Polly?

Mrs Crusoe Oh, this is nice! I've always wanted to go on a luxury cruise. Sitting at the Captain's table, and all that! (*seeing the Captain*) Oh there you are steward. Direct me to the swimming pool please? Is it up the strict end?

Captain Strict end? <u>Stern</u> end, you silly old...

Mrs Crusoe Stern, strict, what's the difference. Is that where the pool is?

Captain I'll direct you to the Galley.

Mrs Crusoe Ah, that's where it is. I hope it's heated.

Captain It will be when you start a' cooking! Ha, ha!

Mrs Crusoe Cooking? Oh I couldn't possibly cook in the swimming pool, you silly boy! All the chips will go soggy! Has it got a nice diving board, and those floating blow-up beds, so that I can relax on the water with my ice cream?

Captain Blow up beds? Crinkle me capstan! What in the Galley? This is a working ship, not a rest home!

Mrs Crusoe Now tell me this Steward. Where do ships go when they're sick?

Captain I dunno. Where do they go?

Mrs Crusoe To the Doc'! Oh! I am a one!

Captain Er! You remind me of the sea Mrs Crusoe.

Mrs Crusoe Oh! You mean I'm all wild, restless, and romantic?

Captain No. The sea makes me feel sick.

Mrs Crusoe Oh I bet you say that to all the girls, you naughty boy! Now I can't stand chatting to you all day, Steward. I've got to practice my breaststroke.

Captain What's she talking about? Breaststroke! I'll stroke you with the cat o' nine tails if you don't start working! The men be getting hungry! (*exits*)

Mrs Crusoe Well! He wasn't very helpful, was he? I'll try over here. (*exits*)

Enter Cedric one side, and the Mate from the other

Cedric Ah Mr Mate! A word if you please, my good man.

Mate Oh. Which word is that then? Here, it's not a rude one is it?

Cedric What? No. This Captain of yours. The one with the big canary what's it.

Mate Yes. The parrot you mean. What about him?

Cedric Well, is he alright? You know trustworthy?

Mate Yes he's alright. He pecks your fingers sometimes though, when you try to give him a nut.

Cedric What? No, no! Not the pelican what's it! I mean the Captain.

Mate Oh! He's alright I suppose - for a pirate.

Cedric WHAT! A pirate! Oh no! We've been captured by pirates! Quick! Sound the alarm or something!

Mate We ain't got no alarm or something.

Cedric Well turn the ship round then. Go back.

Mate I can't do that! The Captain wouldn't like it.

Cedric Perhaps we could swim ashore. How far is it?

Mate Only about twenty miles.

Cedric Forget that then. What sort of things does he do, this pirate chappie?

Mate Oh he sinks ships, strings people up to the yard-arm. Makes people walk the plank, locks them in the bilges with the rats, and all that. Just normal, routine pirate stuff.

Cedric Normal! You call that normal!

Mate Well he's got to do it, otherwise they won't let him be a pirate no more. He'd be thrown out of the pirate's union.

Captain *(entering)* Here! What you two layabouts doing? Get to work.

Mate Aye, aye Captain. *(hurries off on the Captain's side)*

Captain *(to audience)* Now's me chance to teach Mr La di da a lesson! 'ere you!

Cedric *(looking round, scared, hoping the Captain isn't speaking to him)* Oh, I say! What me?

Captain Yes you. Come 'ere.

Cedric *(coming over, hesitantly, to Captain)* Yes Captain?

Captain You ain't been to sea before, have you?

Cedric No Captain.

Captain Well I got a little job for you to do.

Cedric Yes Captain.

Captain Have you seen the crow's nest.

Cedric *(looking round)* No Captain. I didn't take it.

Captain *(looking straight up)* It's up there.

Cedric *(looking straight up, getting dizzy, and holding on to the Captain to steady himself)* What that little thing, right at the top of that mast there?

Captain That's it lad. I can see you're a quick learner. You know what I wants you to do?

Cedric I'm trying not to think about it.

Captain I built that crow's nest, so that I could have fresh eggs for breakfast see. The crow lays 'em special for me. Go up there and bring one down.

Cedric *(looking round)* Where's the lift?

Captain Lift! You'll get a lift if I gets near you wi' the cat o' nine tails! You climbs up the rigging there. *(pointing off stage)*

Cedric What! Up that string stuff? You cannot be serious! I can't stand heights. Wouldn't you like some cornflakes instead?

Captain Look sharp. Or you'll be sleeping wi' the fishes! (*pointing off stage again*) Up that rigging now lad. And don't <u>hang</u> about! Ha, ha! <u>Don't hang about!</u> 'ear that one Polly?

Cedric (*goes off stage*) Oh alright.

Captain (*watching his imagined ascent*) That'll teach 'im, eh Polly? Ha, ha! Mr La di da! Ooh look, he's gone all green!

Cedric (*off, and muffled*) HELP! I'm dizzy!

Enter Robinson

Robinson Captain. I was looking for Cedric.

Captain He's busy. I've promoted him, you see.

Robinson Really! Already?

Captain Oh yes. (*pointing upwards*) He's gone up in the world! Ha, ha! Ain't that right Polly?

Robinson Oh good. I'm glad to hear it.

Captain (*looking up*) He's not far away. He should be <u>dropping in</u> any minute!

Robinson You are in a good mood Captain.

Enter Cedric, briskly, carrying a frying pan with a fried egg in it

Cedric There you are Captain! One fried crow's egg, sunny side up. As ordered.

Captain (*completely taken aback, and taking the frying pan*) What?

Cedric Let me know if you want any more. Lovely view from up there old boy.

Captain Er. I've just gone off me food! I got work to do. (*exits, with frying pan*)

Cedric Robinson. Listen. We're in danger. I've found out that our Captain here is really a pirate.

Robinson A pirate! Then we <u>are</u> in danger. We must do something.

Cedric Yes. But what?

Robinson We're going to have to take over the ship.

Cedric If you say so Robinson.

Robinson Now. here's what we do. You find out how many of the crew are on our side. I'll go and find out where the weapons are locked up.

Cedric Right Robinson. What about the Mate? He might give us some trouble.

Robinson Yes. The Mate. Ah! I've got an idea. You leave him to me. See you back here in a couple of minutes.

Cedric Right. (*exits*)

Enter Mrs Crusoe

Robinson Mother, just the person I was looking for.

Mrs Crusoe Yes. What is it?

Robinson Mother, we're all in danger.

Mrs Crusoe Danger!

Robinson Yes. No time to explain now. Have you got any of that home made wine you brought on board? The really strong stuff?

Mrs Crusoe (*producing a bottle from under her apron*) Of course dear. I never go anywhere without it.

Robinson (*taking the bottle*) Good. Now, find Rosie, and stay together.

Mrs Crusoe Right dear. Oh, isn't this exciting? (*exits*)

Enter the Mate with a piece of rope. He is busy trying to tie a knot

Robinson (*seeing the Mate*) Everything's going to plan. There you are Mr Mate.

Mate (*fiddling with his rope*) Oh, hello.

Robinson (*holding out the bottle*) I've got you a present.

Mate (*looking at the bottle*) What is it?

Robinson It's a special drink. My mother makes it from oranges. Try some.

Mate Oh. I like orange juice. (*he takes a sip*) Cor! It's strong. (*takes another sip*) It's nice. I like it. (*takes another sip*)

Robinson It's all yours. Help yourself.

Mate Thank you. (*drinks again*) It's lovely.

Robinson What are you doing with that rope?

Mate Oh, I'm trying to tie a leaf knot. (*takes another, longer drink*)

Robinson A leaf knot? Ah! You mean a <u>reef</u> knot.

Mate Yes. That's what I said. I'm tying to try a leaf knot. (*takes another swig*)

Robinson (*to the audience*) I don't think he's going to give us any trouble! Now I must keep an eye on the Captain.

Mate (*drunkenly confidential*) Don't worry about him. I've just seen him.

Robinson Have you?

Mate Yes. I popped up to the poopdeck, peeped, and popped down again.

Robinson He won't be able to say that in a minute!

Mate I won't be able to say anything in a minute.

Robinson Now, I must gather up the men. (*exits*)

Mate (*alone on stage*) You know something Sob-inson, you're a good chap you are. You help me tie this beef cake, leaf swot. (*looks around, now drunk*) Where you gone? I know, you're hiding. I'll count up to a hundred? (*starts counting on his fingers*) One, two, three... (*sinks down against the proscenium arch, with his bottle, and counts quietly to himself, oblivious of the following action*)

Robinson re-enters, wearing a sword, also Cedric, and a group of the chorus,
who constitute those loyal to Robinson

Song No 6

This starts as a small chorus number, 'When the Foeman Bears his Steel,
Taran-tara, Taran-tara'. (Pirates of Penzance) The dancers enter with caution,
looking around, with guns and daggers drawn. A dance routine, is incorporated
with the song, that involves searching everywhere, up and down stage etc.,

All   When the foeman bears his steel,
                     Taran-tara, taran-tara.
                     We uncomfortable feel. Taran-tara.
                     And we find the wisest thing,
                     Taran-tara, taran-tara.
                     Is to slap our chests and sing. Taran-tara.
                     For we've got to stop these brutes.
                     Taran-tara, taran-tara.
                     Though our hearts are in our boots. Taran-tara.
                     But there's nothing brings us round,
                     Like the trumpet's martial sound.
                     Like the trumpet's martial sound!
                     Taran-tara, taran-tara, ra, ra, ra, ra,
                     Taran-tara, taran-tara, ra, ra, ra, ra,
                     Taran-tara.

This now expands to a full chorus number as the Captain enters, with cutlass
in hand, and his half of the crew, loyal to him. The opposing parties now face
each other across the stage. Robinson's group stand, waving threateningly, as
the Captain's group sing their verse

                     There is mut'ny on me ship,
                     Taran-tara, taran-tara.
                     And I'm here to punish it. Taran-tara.
                     And for you the wisest thing.
                     Taran-tara, taran-tara.
                     Is to on me mercy fling.
                     Taran-tara.
                     All the leaders of this rout.
                     Taran-tara, taran-tara.
                     So I can cut their livers out. Taran-tara.

Groups sing and march between each other, returning to their original positions

> But there's nothing brings us round,
> Like the trumpet's martial sound.
> Like the trumpet's martial sound!
> Taran-tara, taran-tara, ra, ra, ra, ra,
> Taran-tara, taran-tara, ra, ra, ra, ra,
> Taran-tara.

If desired, the two groups may now sing a final verse. Each half singing their own lines, in opposition to the other half, while they face each other, or march between each other, ending closer together. Glowering at their enemies

At the end of the song, the Mate, who has been quietly finishing his wine, is heard to be slowly counting

Mate Seventy seven, seventy eight, seventy...
Robinson (*drawing sword*) Captain. I arrest you for piracy on the high seas.
Captain Ha, ha! D'you 'ear that Polly? Don't make me laugh lad.
Cedric Give up Captain old boy.
Captain (*flourishing his cutlass*) To the death Robinson.
Robinson Just you and me Captain.
Captain Just you and me then lad.

They circle each other, deadly serious. The chorus cheer their champions. They make a couple of lunges at each other. Suddenly, lights flash, thunder rolls

Mate (*suddenly jumping*) Er! What's that?
Captain A fierce storm a brewin'.
Cedric We must attend to the ship.
Robinson Captain, we must finish this later. The safety of the crew comes first.

Rosie and Mrs Crusoe run on stage

Rosie Robinson! What's happening?
Robinson A great storm is blowing up mother.
Mrs Crusoe Help! Where's the life guard?
Cedric You mean the life belt.
Mrs Crusoe I know what I mean!
Robinson Get them below Cedric.
Mate Eighty nine, ninety.

Cedric takes Mrs Crusoe and Rosie off stage, as Robinson helps the Captain

Captain (*forgetting the quarrel*) Me ship! We've gotta save the ship! All 'ands on deck! Batten down the 'atches! (*to Robinson*) See to that rigging lad! (*he points off stage*)
Robinson (*as he exits*) Aye, aye Captain.
Captain To your duties!

The crew now run about, on and off stage, shouting, some screaming, frantically trying to save the ship. General lights dim as the storm grows. The thunder rolls get louder. The lightning flashes more intense

Captain (*taking up centre stage, pointing, shouting orders, and looking aloft*) Avast there! To the mainmast! Over there! Cut 'er loose there! (*runs off stage pushing the crew out of his way. He can be heard shouting orders off stage*)

The crew continue to work frantically, as the storm reaches its climax

Captain (*returning*) Tis no use! She's sinking. Abandon ship! Abandon ship! She's goin' down! Man the life boats!
Mate Ninety nine, hundred. Coming! (*staggers off stage*)

The crew begin to panic. There is more running and shouting as the lights slowly dim, and the curtains close

Scene 4

This is an interact scene to facilitate the changing of scenery. It can be played in front of tabs, or a frontcloth showing an ocean sea bed

Enter Queen Neptune and a sea-creature assistant. There is an angry rumbling sound

Queen Neptune (*looking around*) Oh dear. What's all that noise?
Assistant I'm afraid it's King Neptune again your majesty.
Queen Neptune How tiresome! Having another one of his moods?
Assistant Afraid so your majesty.
Queen Neptune I suppose his favourite team Liver-pool (*or local team*) lost again?
Assistant Three nil your majesty.
Queen Neptune Dear me. This is really too much.

Assistant Yes. They'll be relegated if they go on like this.

Queen Neptune No. I didn't mean... I hope there aren't any ships in the area.

Assistant The Electric Eel picked up a distress signal from one your majesty.

Queen Neptune Oh, I'll have to entertain the crew I suppose. Make amends for my bad-tempered husband. See what you can rustle up from the freezer.

Assistant It'll have to be the fish fingers again. Sainsburys is shut now. Shall I send the crew in when they arrive? *(exits)*

Queen Neptune Yes I suppose so. *(picks up a clipboard with, 'Neptune's Tours' on the front)* That's the knitting circle cancelled again. I'll never get those leggings for Olly the Octopus finished. I hope the ship doesn't land in my new flower beds. I've only just put the sea anemones in.

Assistant returns with Captain and Mate, who has arrows in his hat, or an Indian head-dress on

Assistant Some of the crew your majesty. *(exits again)*

Captain *(looking at the Mate's head)* Where's that come from?

Mate *(looking up)* We must be in the Indian Ocean!

Captain Curry me compasses! Look at this! We're in Davy Jones' locker!

Mate *(looking round)* Got a bit of a damp problem, ain't they boss?

Captain It won't affect you. You're always wet! Ha, ha!

Mate Your Polly's gone all soggy boss! He, he!

Queen Neptune Ah. Hello. Welcome to the wonderful underwater world of King Neptune. I'm Queen Neptune, your guide on this tour. This is our ancient ruined city here, as you can see. We're rather proud of it. Now try to keep together, and don't wander off on your own. *(to audience)* Oh I wish I didn't have to do this. The place is getting like Woburn Abbey! *(to Captain)* Can I get you a glass of air? I know you Earth-thingys are rather fond of the stuff.

Captain No thanks gel. Ain't you got nothing a bit stronger?

Queen Neptune Well I can get you some nice herbal seaweed tea.

Captain Muzzle me mainmast! That sounds revolting!

Queen Neptune It's very refreshing. We've gone very health food conscious down here you see. Were there any more of your crew on the way?

Captain Oh yes. They're <u>floating</u> around somewhere! He, he! <u>Floating around somewhere!</u> He, he! What d'you think o' that one eh Polly? Who's a clever... Oh shut your face.

Cedric *(entering, wearing wellies, fisherman's hat and carrying a fishing net)* I say! Look at this <u>fishy plaice</u>! I'm not here o-<u>fish</u>-ially, but I'm having a <u>whale</u> of a time! A fish tried to lend me money out there. It was a <u>loan-shark</u>! But I showed him a bit of <u>mussel</u>, and he <u>dived</u> off! That long thin fish looked a bit down at <u>eel</u> to me, or was he a <u>red herring</u>? I've bought a fine <u>tuna</u> for my radio, paid for it in <u>gold</u> fish. Oh, I think I'll have a lie down on the <u>sea bed</u>!

Enter Rosie and Robinson

Robinson Look at all this Rosie.
Rosie I wonder what the water rates are?
Robinson What an adventure! (*noticing Queen Neptune*) Look, who's that?
Queen Neptune Hello. I'm Queen Neptune. Some more of the crew. Good.

Enter Mrs Crusoe with an umbrella up, wearing flippers, snorkel mask, and a plastic mack

Mrs Crusoe So this is Manchester! Well! I knew it was wet, but this is ridiculous!
Queen Neptune Welcome to the ancient old ruin.
Mrs Crusoe Here! Do you mind!
Queen Neptune Do join us.
Mrs Crusoe It must be like living in a gold-fish bowl down here!
Robinson Mother. Come over here.
Mrs Crusoe Ah there you are Robinson. Now don't get your feet wet. You know how easy you catch cold.
Cedric Glad to see you're safe Mrs C.
Mrs Crusoe Safe! A crab just bit my toe out there!
Queen Neptune (*looking down at her feet*) Really, which one?
Mrs Crusoe I don't know. All crabs look the same to me!
Queen Neptune (*to audience*) There's always one, isn't there?
Mrs Crusoe Oh I could murder a sardine sandwich!

A chorus of shocked gasps

Queen Neptune Well! Now that we're all here, shall we go through?

The curtains slowly open

Scene 5

King Neptune's Throne Room. The backcloth should show a seabed with; debris from wrecks, rocks, coral, seaweed etc., The remains of an ancient underwater ruin, complete with a throne. Some of the chorus, dressed as sea creatures, are wandering around, and stationary. There should be items that the Captain and Mate can search through, plus something for Olly the Octopus to hide behind (the throne may serve for this)

Cast move back into throne room, led by Queen Neptune, who has Mrs Crusoe's umbrella, rolled it down, and holding it over her head like a tour guide

Queen Neptune Follow me everyone. It's easy to get lost. Keep your eyes on the umbrella, and keep together. *(leads the group over to one side of the stage)*

Group chatter quietly, admiring what they see

Now here we have the ancient underwater city that you Earth-thingys call Atlantis. Second century, Greek origin. The throne is rather interesting. One of a pair originally said to belong to Queen Nefertiti. On we go. *(leads the group off stage, as they look round)* Over here we have a genuine Roman galley, sunk in 49 AD. Do keep together! It still has some interesting markings...

The sea creatures gather for their dance. Those on stage, and stationary, begin to move slowly, as the UV lamp comes up. They will be joined by others from the wings. They should be dressed as; starfish, sea anemones, shells, octopi, fish, lobsters, crabs, pieces of coral etc.,

Music No 7

The dance of the sea creatures. A junior ballet number. The lights dim, a UV fluorescent lamp comes up. The use of whites on the costumes, and backcloth, will help to give this dance a magical atmosphere

Either to the theme music from 'The Onedin Line' or 'The Octopus's Garden' or 'La Mer' or another appropriate, slow piece of music, ballet or otherwise, the junior chorus perform a slow, graceful dance routine. Alternatively, they could dance a lively hornpipe

At the end of the dance most of the chorus exit. Some may stay to take up stationary positions on the stage. The lights come up a little

Enter Captain and Mate

Captain Here we are then Matey.
Mate But she told us to all stay together!

Captain Never mind her Matey. Now look round here.

Mate What we looking for?

Captain This is Davy Jones' locker!

Mate What's that?

Captain Burnish me bowline! You be a sailor and you don't know that?

Mate Nope.

Captain Davy Jones were a pirate you see...

Mate Oh, like you?

Captain (*looking round*) Easy Matey, easy! Walls have ears - even seawalls! Ha, ha! What d'you think o' that one eh Polly?

Mate What about this Davy Jones, one time pirate?

Captain One time! All the time Matey! Ha, ha!

Mate I think we're stuck here for ever!

Captain Now, listen carefully. I shall say this only once! Now, this Davy Jones, his ship sank you see. With all his treasure. Down here. That's why they call the bottom of the sea, Davy Jones' locker. Where he stashed all his loot.

Mate (*looking round*) You mean it's all down here, somewhere?

Captain Yes! That's why we gotta find it. So start looking.

Mate Are you sure it's alright? I saw some funny things floating around when we came in.

Captain That's just the Queen, hung out her washing, I expect.

Mate (*looking round*) What! She don't expect it to dry here, does she?

Captain Will you stop moaning and search?

Mate Here boss. Who do you think is the best actor down here?

Captain I dunno.

Mate The STAR-fish! He, he!

Captain SEARCH!

They begin to look around

Mate (*after a very brief look, and loudly*) It's not here. Can we go out now?

Captain Will you be quiet! Someone'll hear you.

Mate (*in a whisper*) Can we go out?

Captain No!

Mate (*loudly*) Why not?

Captain Give me strength! Look over there.

The Mate looks around and picks up a tin of cat food

Mate (*loudly*) What's this tin of Whiskas doing here?

Captain It's for the cat fish. Shhh!

Mate (*putting tin down again*) Oh. NOTHING ELSE HERE!

Captain I'll murder 'im in a minute! So 'elp me!

Mate (*loudly*) Boss I bet you don't know the proper name for a mermaid.

Captain Will you be quiet! Er. What's the use!

Mate A deep <u>SHE</u> fish! He, he! Good ain't it?

Captain Do you know something Matey.

Mate What's that boss?

Captain If you donated your brain to medical science, they could put it in a match box, and it'd still rattle about!

Mate Oh, thanks boss.

Captain Come 'ere.

Mate WHAT?

Captain (*with exaggerated sweetness*) I said 'Come over here and help me'.

Mate (*noticing the sweetness, and tiptoeing over to the Captain, like a ballet dancer*) Oh! Of course Captain. You're the boss.

When he arrives the Captain sloshes him with his hat

Captain You great fool! Be quiet when I tells you! You look there. I'm going to look in here. (*points off stage*)

Mate (*grabbing hold of the Captain tightly*) Oh, don't leave me on me own boss.

Captain (*struggling to be free*) Will you get off me!

Mate (*still holding on*) No boss. Suppose something big and horrible comes in?

Captain Too late Matey. You're already here! Ha, ha! Just tell 'em one o' your jokes. They'll die laughing!

Captain struggles free and exits

Mate Yes. That's a good idea. I'll tell them the one about - what ship can't sail? A town-ship. He, he! No, that's no good. I got to think of a good one. I know. This is a good one. This man see, he said to the other man see, 'That's a nasty bite you've got on the top of your head'. So the other man, the one with the bite see, he said, 'Yes, I bit meself'. So the other man said, 'Bit yourself? How could you bite yourself up there?' So the man with the bite said, 'I stood on a ladder!' He, he! I wonder if a shark would laugh at that?

Enter Olly the Octopus behind the Mate

I don't like it in here on my own. You will tell me if something fishy turns up, won't you?

Audience It's behind you!

Mate What?
Audience It's behind you!
Mate It's not is it? You're just trying to frighten me.

Olly comes closer

Audience It's behind you!
Mate Alright then. I'm, I'm, going to be very b-b-brave. I'm going to look.

Olly hides. Mate looks round

There's nothing there! You tricked me!

Olly appears again

Audience It's behind you!
Mate No it's not.
Audience Yes it is!

Olly comes closer

Mate Where?
Audience Behind you!
Mate Alright I'm going to look again, and this time I'm going to keep my eyes open as well, so it had better be there. Oh no. I mean, it had better not be there. Oh, I don't know.

Olly hides. Mate looks round

Mate There's nothing there. I knew it. I wasn't scared anyway. I'm brave I am. I'm as brave as Colonel Custard I am.

Olly returns

Audience It's behind you!

Olly is now right behind him, and touches him on the shoulder

Mate Ow, er! What's that?

He turns and Olly waves at him

OH! HELP! I WANT ME MUM!

He runs off stage. Olly waves to the audience and then hides again. The Captain returns

Captain There's nothing in there. (*looks around*) Where's he gone now? (*to audience*) Where did he go?

Gets a variety of responses from the audience to make sense of

What, run away? Was he scared o' something then?
Audience Yes!
Captain What was it?
Audience An octopus!
Captain A Red Line Bus?
Audience An octopus.
Captain A rhino-roceros?
Audience An octopus!
Captain An octopus! One o' them titchy little octopussy things?
Audience Yes!

Olly appears behind Captain

Captain Cor! Bust me britches! Fancy being scared o' one o' them! He'll never get to be a captain, being scared like that! Where is it now?
Audience It's behind you!
Captain (*suddenly not so sure*) What right behind me? It's not is it?
Audience Yes!
Captain Tell it to go away then.
Audience No!
Captain Go on you rotten lot. Tell it.
Audience NO!

Captain slowly looks round, sees Olly, and runs, followed by Olly

Captain HELP! Let's get out of 'ere Polly!

Enter Queen Neptune, Rosie and Robinson

Queen Neptune So Mrs Crusoe's husband just disappeared?
Robinson Yes.

Queen Neptune How strange! Mind you, I sometimes wish mine would! He can be so bad-tempered at times. And this Bossalot woman, forced you and your poor mother out of your house, because you two were in love?

Robinson I'm afraid it's true, your majesty.

Queen Neptune You have had a difficult time of it. Such strange behaviour Bossalot, and you Earth-thingys have.

Rosie Only some, not all.

Queen Neptune Yes, well, I should certainly hope not. She should be punished. I do have some powers you know. At least as far as the sea is concerned.

Robinson Oh, but we wouldn't want her to be hurt.

Rosie No.

Queen Neptune Well, I'll see what can be arranged. Ah here comes Olly, my pet octopus. Have you met him yet?

Olly enters, and Robinson and Rosie turn to meet him

Rosie Oh isn't he sweet? Hello Olly.

Robinson Hello Olly.

Rosie Have you said hello to the children yet?

Olly indicates 'no'

Would you like to?

Olly indicates 'yes'

(to audience) Say hello to Olly.

Audience Hello Olly.

Olly waves back

Rosie There. Where are your friends Olly?

Olly indicates off stage

Robinson Can we meet them?

Olly says 'yes'

Rosie *(to audience)* You'd like to meet them, wouldn't you?

Audience Yes.

Olly signals, and the sea creatures enter, waving to the audience. Rosie and Robinson now shake hands with the sea creatures, and chat to them. While they are occupied, Queen Neptune comes forward and talks to the audience

Queen Neptune Such nice people. *(to audience)* Shall I try to help them?
Audience Yes.
Queen Neptune They need money to get married. So I'll arrange for them to be delivered to a nice island, and I'll wash up some treasure on the beach for them to find. Yes. <u>And</u> they'll find something else as well. Something they don't expect to find. But I'll keep that a secret for now.. As for that Bossalot woman! She deserves to be punished. Well! I must go. I <u>have</u> lots to do! Bye! *(waves to audience and exits)*

TABLEAU.

Robinson and Rosie now come forward and prepare the audience for the Community Number

Rosie Would you like to sing a song with our friends?
Audience Yes.
Robinson Good. Now we're all together we can have a party for Olly.
Rosie We've got some words here to help you.

Words can be brought on, by members of the chorus. Or included in the programme, as a song sheet

Song No 8

House song. 'Three Little Fishes' or 'Tiptoe through the Seaweed' or 'If You go Down to the Sea Today' to the tune of 'The Teddy Bear's Picnic'

If the latter is chosen, the following words are suggested

> If you go down to the sea today,   ,
> You're sure of a big surprise.
> If you go down to the sea today,
> You'd better go in disguise.
> For everything that knows how to swim,
> Is gathered there to kick up a din.
> Today's the day the Octopus has his party.

At the end of the song, curtain. End of Act 1. **Interval**

ACT 2

Robinson Crusoe's Camp. Backcloth should show a picture-book beach scene, with palm trees, blue sea, golden beach, Crusoe's hut, fire, and a collection of debris; boxes, barrels etc., rescued from the ship etc., On stage should be a couple of seats/benches

As the curtains open, the female chorus are on stage, and dressed as island natives, in grass skirts etc., wearing slightly darker make-up. They sing and dance

Song No 9

'We're Having a Heatwave' or 'Oh Island in the Sun' or another

At the end of the song, enter Robinson and Man Friday

Robinson I'm glad I found you on this island, Man Friday. You've been a great help. I don't know what I'd do without you?
Man Friday Yep positive guv.
Robinson With your help, and good old Cedric, we'll have the boat finished in no time. Then we can get off this island, and go back home.
Man Friday You take me with you guv?
Robinson Of course, if that's what you want.
Man Friday Yep positive guv. Me play for Manchester United. *(produces a Man Utd football scarf and puts it on)*
Robinson I was forgetting your ambition to play football, Man Friday.
Man Friday Man Friday short for Man United Friday guv. Me brother he supports a different team - so - me Man United Friday - and him Sheffield Wednesday.

Enter Cedric

Cedric I've put the flag pole up, like you said, Robinson.
Robinson Good. Did you find something large and white to hang from it, for a signal? In case any ships pass by.
Cedric I hung up the largest white things that I could find. But I don't know what Mrs C will say when she finds out!
Robinson What do you mean?

Man Friday He means he hung up her bloomers, guv.

Robinson I think we'd better get out of here, before she comes back.

Cedric Good idea, let's go and work on the boat.

Man Friday Yep positive guv.

Robinson and Cedric exit, Man Friday is picking up some tools as Rosie and Mrs Crusoe enter. Mrs Crusoe has the sock she was knitting earlier in Act 1, it has now grown to enormous proportions

Mrs Crusoe I can't understand it! I had them on yesterday! They must be around somewhere.

Man Friday (*laughing*) Yep. They must be <u>hanging</u> about somewhere! (*exits quickly*)

Mrs Crusoe How does he know what I'm looking for? There's a cruel draft blowing though the bamboos I can tell you! Oh, I'm sick of knitting this sock!

Rosie Surely it's long enough now, why don't you cast off?

They sit down

Mrs Crusoe The trouble is nobody told me how to! Still, he'll grow into it.

Rosie Grow into it! He'll probably suffocate in it! You'd better make it into a sleeping bag!

Mrs Crusoe Robinson's gone off working on his boat again I suppose?

Rosie Yes. He says it's nearly finished.

Mrs Crusoe Thank goodness! I can't wait to get home and find out what's happening in East Enders!

Enter Captain and Mate, who is carrying a shovel

Captain Pieces of eight! Pieces of eight! Who's a pretty boy? Who's a pretty boy then? You are! You are! Ha, ha!

Rosie Have you been helping Robinson with the boat?

Captain Oh no. We've been digging for buried treasure. Bound to be some around here somewheres. Just the sort o' place they used to bury it you see. Been digging all mornin' we 'ave.

Mate (*holding up shovel*) Well I have anyway. (*he puts the shovel down*)

Rosie You won't find any. You'd be better off helping Robinson build his boat. The sooner we get off this island the better. Everyone's bored.

Captain They're <u>bored</u>, so they want to be on-<u>board</u>! Ha! What d'you think o' that one eh Polly?

Rosie I'll tell you what I think. You should be helping us to escape.

Captain Ah well I'm used to a more supervisory position you see. Me being a Captain an' all. Brainwork is more in my style. I should a' taken that job with Sealink. Probably be driving an 'overcraft by now.

Mate What's brainwork boss?

Captain Er! Questions, questions! Brainwork is what <u>you</u> can't do for a start! It's when you sit around with your eyes closed - thinking - planning - and all that. O' course a couple of beers helps to get things started like. Settles your brain down a treat, that does.

Mate Oh. Like when you're snoring after dinner?

Captain That's right. O' course it ain't <u>real</u> snoring you see. It's kind of pretend snoring - all part of the delicate process, you see.

Mate That don't sound too hard. I think I could do that.

Captain No, takes years o' dedicated practice lad. Ain't that right Polly old girl?

Rosie and Mrs Crusoe listen with incredulity at the Mate's simplicity

Mrs Crusoe (*getting up*) I can't stand any more of this. I'll get the dinner ready.

Rosie I'll help you.

They both exit

Captain (*looking round to make sure that the coast is clear*) Now lad, have you found that map yet?

Mate No boss. I don't think they've got one.

Captain O' course they 'ave. It's carefully hidden. They plan to finish the boat, you see. Then they'll get the treasure - scarpa - and leave us here -stranded.

Mate Ooh! That'll be nice boss. We could have a holiday here, all on our own. I could make up some picnics for the beach.

Captain (*taking his hat off and hitting the Mate with it*) Blister me barnacles! Do you think I want to be stuck on this deserted island with a fool like you?

Mate But the boat's nearly finished, so they'll be away soon.

Captain Ah, that's where me genius comes in useful.

Mate What you mean boss?

Captain Well, every day they do a bit o' work on the boat see?

Mate That's right.

Captain And every night I gets up and undoes it!

Mate What for?

Captain To slow 'em down! Til we find the map! Now if you'd been real management material, which you ain't, you'd 'ave thought of that!

Mate Perhaps I should go on one of them management courses.

Captain Huh! That'd be a right waste o' money!

Mate But boss. If they haven't got a map. We could be here forever, if you keep undoing the boat every night.

Captain They've got a map, I keep tellin' yer! It's 'idden somewheres.

Mate Ah! But where? You don't know do you?

Captain That's where you're wrong again Matey! I reckon that Mrs Crusoe's got it hidden about her person somewhere.

Mate We'll never find it then. Nobody's ever going to look for it there.

Captain stands to attention and salutes, as a heroic march, Dambusters, or whatever, comes up, slowly

Captain (*over the music*) Matey, I must make a great sacrifice. There comes a time when a man's gotta do, what a man's gotta do! This calls for bravery above and beyond the call o' duty. Never in the field of 'uman conflict, has one man given so much, for so little. I shall fight 'er on the beaches, I shall... (*the music suddenly dies*) Hey up. Here she comes now, so clear off and leave me some room to work in. I'll try me masculine charm on 'er. Ha! Never fails that.

Mate Righto then boss. Good luck. (*exits*)

Captain Now I'll just hide 'ere for a minute. keep an eye on 'er, just to make sure she's in the right sort o' mood for what I 'ave in mind. (*moves to the wings and peers out at her*)

Enter Mrs Crusoe, with a mixing bowl that contains shaving cream, or something that can be poured over the Captain's head. she puts the bowl down, and picks it up again after her solo number

Mrs Crusoe Oh I wish I was home - somewhere comfortable - like a mansion, surrounded by servants, riches, piles of gold, you know, just the simple things that make life bearable.

Song No 10

A solo from Mrs Crusoe. 'An Old-Fashioned Millionaire' or 'Diamonds are a Girl's Best Friend' or 'All I Want is a Room Somewhere' or another

At the end of the song, Captain enters

Captain (*to the audience*) Here we go then. Now to find the map. (*to Mrs Crusoe*) Ah there you are Mrs C. Come over here and rest your legs for a bit.

Mrs Crusoe For a bit of what?

He makes an exaggerated play of brushing a seat clean with his hat. Mrs Crusoe treats his attentions with deep suspicion as she sits down

Captain Cooking us something delicious again for dinner Mrs C. I don't know 'ow you does it. Straight up I don't.

Mrs Crusoe Well I am having a little trouble getting me Yorkshire puddings to rise.

Captain Perhaps they're a bit tired eh? Always been an early riser meself. You fair warms a poor old sailor's 'eart, that you do. Ain't that right Polly? *(walks round behind her, looking for possible places where the map might be hidden)*

Mrs Crusoe *(following his movements with her eyes, carefully)* Oh!

Captain *(sitting down beside her and puts his arm behind her)* Ha, ha! I like the cut of your jib, Mrs C!

Mrs Crusoe *(jumping as he touches her, and looking behind her)* Really! I didn't know it was showing!

Captain *(moving in closer)* You're a very 'andsome lady, if you'll pardon a sailor's boldness, Mrs C.

Mrs Crusoe Oh don't! You'll have me all of a doo daa!

Again background music comes up. This time it is 'There's no Place like Home'

Captain *(over the music)* A man who's spent his life at sea, he gets lonely for some home comforts, Mrs C. Yes. The warm smile that greets 'im at the end o' the day. The patter o' tiny feet. Slippers by the fireside. The smell o' bread, bakin' in the oven.

They are lost in a moment of pure nostalgia. The music dies. His hands begin to move about behind her as she squirms and wriggles

Mrs Crusoe *(suddenly breaking the atmosphere)* You naughty boy! Stop that!

Captain *(moving away, and taking his arm away)* Beggin' your pardon Mrs C.

Mrs Crusoe *(moving close to him, and putting his arm back where it was)* Only joking, you silly boy!

Captain *(pulling a face)* I should get a medal for this! Ha, ha! You're not ticklish are you? *(returns to his search)*

Mrs Crusoe *(struggling)* Now I know why all pirates are like contortionists! And it's not because they can sit on their chests!

Captain I like a woman wi' a sense of 'umour! Ha, ha!

Mrs Crusoe Oh don't! You'll squash me Yorkshires! *(to audience)* He'll be showing me his engagement ring in a minute!

The Mate appears and stays half-hidden in the wings, on the Captain's side

Mate (*whispering to the Captain*) The shoes boss. Look in the shoes.

Captain What? Oh yes. (*lifts her skirt slightly to see her shoes*)

Mrs Crusoe HERE! What do you think you're doing! Get off!

Captain (*to Mate*) Plaster me Poopdeck! She could get the Encyclopedia Brittanica in these! I've 'eard of the Blackfoot tribe. She must be from the Bigfoot tribe!

Mrs Crusoe (*defending herself, and hitting him with the stirring spoon*) Stop this immediately! Help!

Captain (*as the shoes come off*) Cor! Anyone got a gas mask?

Mrs Crusoe Get away! How dare you! Leave my feet alone!

Captain Your shoes need a bit o' mendin' Mrs C. The Mate'll see to it.

Mrs Crusoe OH! HELP!

To bangs and crashes, the Captain takes her shoes off, roughly, and throws them to the Mate, hiding, half out of the wings

Have a look in them quick.

Mate (*quickly looking in the shoes and throwing them back to the Captain*) Nothing boss.

Captain (*as the shoes hit him*) Ouch! Be careful you fool! You sure? It must be hidden somewhere else then. (*gets up to go*)

Mrs Crusoe (*putting one of her shoes on*) Here! You're not going are you? Aren't you going to ask for my telephone number or anything? (*to audience*) Well! He went off the boil a bit quick!

Captain Stop prattlin' you old crow. I'm trying to think.

Mrs Crusoe WHAT? OLD CROW AM I? Well here's some of those home comforts you were wanting. (*to a crash, she pours the contents of the mixing bowl over his head and exits, limping with only one shoe on*)

Captain (*tasting the liquid with his fingers*) Polly! We've been poisoned! (*exits towards the Mate*) This is all your fault you fool!

Half in and half out of the wings, the Captain can be seen hitting the Mate. Bangs and crashes as Mate yells

Mate (*hidden, as the Captain hits him*) Ouch! Ooh! Help!

When they have gone, enter Robinson and Man Friday

Robinson I can't understand it. I'm sure we did that bit of planking yesterday.

Man Friday It's the sun, you're not used to it.

Robinson Do you think so?

Man Friday Yep, positive.

Enter Cedric

Robinson Not seen any ships, I suppose?

Cedric Not a sausage old boy.

Rosie *(entering)* Hello. Finished for the day then?

Robinson Yes finished Rosie.

Rosie I wonder if we'll ever get off this island?

Robinson Of course we will.

Cedric It is nice here, but I wouldn't want to stay forever.

Rosie No.

Cedric If we do get off, one day, I suppose we'll all go in different directions. Perhaps never see each other again.

Robinson Don't say that Cedric. *(looking around at all of them)* After all we've been through! We're a team.

Man Friday Like Man United! Yep positive!

Robinson We stick together.

Man Friday Does that include me guv?

Robinson Yep positive.

Song No 11

A quartet from Robinson, Rosie, Cedric and Man Friday. 'Whatever We Do, Wherever We Go' or 'Consider Yourself at Home' or 'Tomorrow' or another

At the end of the song

Rosie *(to Robinson)* Let's go for a walk along the beach before dinner.

Robinson Good idea. See you later folks.

Robinson and Rosie exit, leaving Cedric and Man Friday on stage

Cedric Now Man Friday, what were you telling me about old Jumble Rumble what's it?

Man Friday Beware of Rumble Tum, big white chief, live on other side of island. Yep positive guv'. If you see him come this way, you run like hell that way.

Cedric Is this jolly Jumble Sale what's it not very civilised then?

Man Friday Oh yes, he very civilised. When Thompson coach arrives, he throws big party. Invite them all for dinner.

Cedric I say! That's sounds like jolly fun. What do they eat?

Man Friday People on coach.

Cedric Yes that's it. What do the people on the coach eat? Is there some traditional meal prepared?

Man Friday Yep positive guv'. It's called Thompson coach party stew.

Cedric That sounds nice. What's in it?

Man Friday You don't want to know.

Cedric I see. Some secret recipe eh? Enough said old boy. What do you think happens to the boat at night?

Man Friday What you mean?

Cedric Well surely you've noticed that when we go to the boat in the morning, the bit we did yesterday has been undone.

Man Friday That is big white spirit of Rumble Tum. Come in night. Not want you to leave until you get invite to dinner. Yep positive guv'.

Cedric Oh! Why doesn't he send the invite over then?

Man Friday Him not hungry yet.

Cedric Do you think so?

Man Friday Yep positive guv'.

Cedric Funny though. I thought I heard someone saying, 'Who's a pretty boy then', down there last night.

Man Friday You not go down at night. Bad medicine guv.

Cedric Bad medicine. What like castor oil you mean?

Man Friday Yep positive guv'. Remember, famous island saying, "When hear tom tom of Rumble Tum, run til your legs is numb".

Cedric I say! That's a bit of a tongue twister. Let's see if I can say it - when hear tom tom of Rumble Tum, run til your legs is numb. Did it! Jolly good one that.

Enter Mrs Crusoe

I say Mrs C. Have you heard this one?

Mrs Crusoe Not now Cedric. I've just had a disaster with me Yorkshires.

Cedric Well then. This is just the sort of what's it to cheer you up. Now, can you say this? Er, when hear tom tom of Rumble Tum, run til your legs is numb.

Mrs Crusoe Cedric, I'm not in the mood for your, 'Tom tom eats chewing gum, that's why his leg's gone numb' jokes.

Cedric Not quite right old girl. Care to try again?

Mrs Crusoe What am I going to do about me Yorkshires?

Cedric Ah. Ended up overcooked?

Mrs Crusoe No. They ended up over the Captain!

Cedric (*to Man Friday*) Time to get washed up for dinner old boy.

Man Friday and Cedric exit

Mrs Crusoe I wonder what he meant, 'Don't eat the chewing gum, it'll make your tom tom go numb?' We haven't got any chewing gum.

Enter Robinson and Rosie running

Robinson Mother! Mother! Guess what?
Mrs Crusoe Oh no - you're not going to tell me about 'Long John eats chewing gum, that's why his leg's gone numb' are you?

Rosie and Robinson look at each other, puzzled

Rosie What?
Robinson No! We've found treasure. A big box of it. Washed up on the shore down there.
Mrs Crusoe Robinson I've had enough silly jokes for one day.
Robinson It's true. Look, we brought back some of the coins. (*holds out a handful of coins*)
Mrs Crusoe There you are then. Like I told you... (*sees the coins*) Ooh! Where did you get these?
Rosie Down there. There's hundred's. WE'RE RICH! WE'RE RICH!
Mrs Crusoe I'M RICH! I'M RICH! (*examines the coins, keeps one, and hands the rest back to Robinson*)

They all cheer. Enter Cedric and Man Friday, running

Cedric What's up?
Man Friday What's all shouting?
Rosie We've found treasure.
Robinson Washed up on the beach, down there. (*passes the coins round to be examined*)
Man Friday You sure rich now guv. Yep positive.

Song No 12 ✗2

A quintet from Robinson, Rosie, Mrs Crusoe, Man Friday and Cedric. 'Money, Money, Money' or 'Money Makes the World go Around' or another

*At the end of the song. Captain and Mate come quietly on stage and listen to
the conversation*

Cedric How much treasure is there?

Robinson There's loads Cedric.

Rosie There's doubloons, pieces of eight, sovereigns, rings, gold jewellery, all
sorts.

Captain (*to the Mate*) Didn't I tell you Matey? I can smell treasure a mile off.
Come on. (*coming forward*) Ah yes. The treasure. I was going to tell you about
that. It must've slipped me mind. It belongs to an old shipmate o' mine. He's
asked us to look after it for him. Yes. Ain't that right eh Polly? That's right!
That's right! Ha, ha!

Robinson I don't believe you.

Captain Aw, ah! Tis true. Old Polly here never tells a lie. Now if you'll just hand
the coins over, careful like...

Robinson No! Tell us what's in the bag of treasure first.

Rosie (*about to correct Robinson*) But Robinson, it's in a...

Robinson signals to her, and she stops, understanding, just in time

Captain (*looking at Rosie, trying to remember what she has just said*) In the
bag eh? Well there's doubloons...

They gather round him now, giving encouragement, in the style of Bruce Forsyth

Robinson Doubloons yes, keep thinking all the time...

Captain (*still looking at Rosie, as they help him on*) Er, pieces of eight,

Cedric Pieces of eight, well done! Yes...

Captain Er rings...

Robinson Don't forget the rings, yes...

Captain Some gold jewellery...

Robinson Gold jewellery! I'm glad you remembered that, yes...

Man Friday Something else!

Robinson Yes something else. What was it?

Captain Sovereigns!

Robinson Sovereigns! Good! Didn't he do well?

A bell rings. They all clap. The Captain looks pleased

Rosie So the stuff in the bag is all yours?

Captain That's right, so if you'll just hand it...

Robinson Well what we found is in a <u>box</u>, so it's nothing to do with you!

Everyone laughs

Captain (*pulling a gun*) Now back off me hearties. Tis time for the Captain here to have the last laugh. Ha, ha!
Robinson You won't get away with this!
Cedric Told you he was a jolly bounder Robinson.

Captain takes the coins from a helpless Robinson. Suddenly there is the sound of tom tom drums

Man Friday Help! Tom toms of Rumble Tum! We're going in the big pot. Not play for Man United! Yep positive!
Mrs Crusoe Going in the big pot? Don't be silly! I had a bath before I left Plymouth! (*comes forward and talks to the audience*) Look! Aren't I the one? (*shows the coin that she kept back*) Old Captain Birdseye missed this one!

Two warriors enter and take the Captain and Mate off, unseen by the rest, who come forward to watch Mrs Crusoe

Mrs Crusoe Now you won't tell him will you? Let's keep it our secret. I wonder how much it's worth? I hope it's not one of those ECU things. They're not worth a lot are they?
Robinson Well done mother.

Two warriors enter and take off Cedric and Man Friday. Mrs Crusoe tests coin by biting it

Mrs Crusoe You know, this is the richest I've been since I won (*local drama club*) raffle ten years ago!

Two warriors enter and take off Robinson and Rosie

Robinson (*as he disappears*) MOTHER!

Mrs Crusoe at last looks round when there is no-one else left

Mrs Crusoe Yes, Robinson? Oh! (*to audience*) Where's everyone gone?

Confused responses from audience which Mrs Crusoe tries to make sense of

What? Playing Hide and Seek?

Audience NO etc.,

Mrs Crusoe What? In the Bermuda Triangle?

Audience NO etc.,

Mrs Crusoe Oh it's like being in that Agatha Christie play! What was it called? You know, the one where everyone disappears, one by one. The Marie Celeste. that was it.

Warriors come for Mrs Crusoe, look at her. Feel her arms and shake heads

Ooh! Who's a big boy then? *(pushing him)* Don't touch the goods unless you're buying mate!

Warrior 1 We not take this one. No good for pot.

They begin to exit

Mrs Crusoe Wait a minute! No you don't! *(she takes hold of them)* If there's a party. count me in! *(drags them off)*

Warrior 1 *(as he is pulled off)* Help! Let me go!

The curtains close

Scene 2

Along the beach. This is an interact scene that may be played in front of tabs, or a frontcloth showing a deserted part of the beach

The warriors enter, and pull Rosie and Robinson across the stage

Robinson Let go of us! Stay close to me Rosie!

Rosie I don't have a lot of choice Robinson!

They exit other side. Pause and enter Mrs Crusoe, being pulled away, in the opposite direction, by the two warriors

Warrior 1 You clear off. We not want you!

There is a pause, then Mrs Crusoe enters, pulling the two warriors

Mrs Crusoe Come along now. Don't be difficult.

Warrior 1 Put us down!

They all exit other side. There is another pause, then Mrs Crusoe enters, this time being pulled away by the two warriors

Warrior 1 You go away.
Mrs Crusoe (*to audience, as she is pulled across the stage*) Oh isn't this fun? Much better than knitting socks!

They exit the other side. Again a slight pause, then Mrs Crusoe drags the two warriors back again

Mrs Crusoe You can't get rid of me as easy as that! (*to audience*) I think I'm winning! (*pauses midway for breath*) Oh, I'm all out of condition! I should have kept up with me callinetics!
Warrior 1 You for Rumble Tum big pot.
Mrs Crusoe Oh! He wants to take me on his big yacht! How romantic! Can I go back for my suntan cream? The sea breeze plays havoc with my delicate complexion!

Warriors try to creep off quietly. Mrs Crusoe spots them and drags them back

Mrs Crusoe No you don't. Now, I'll tell you what I'll do. I'll let you go if you can answer an easy riddle?
Warrior 1 You sure riddle easy?
Mrs Crusoe Now, would I try to trick you?

The warriors look at each other, then nod emphatically

Mrs Crusoe Oh no I wouldn't.
Warrior 1 Oh yes you would!
Mrs Crusoe Now don't start that again. Now. If it takes ten men a week to build a wall. How long would it take five men to build it?
Warrior 1 Ah! Two weeks.
Mrs Crusoe Wrong! None! The ten men have already built it!
Warrior 1 Run for it!

The warriors run off stage

Mrs Crusoe Come back here, you lost! (*runs after them*)

When the stage is empty the curtains open

Scene 3

Camp of King Rumble Tum. Backcloth should show a dense forest, mountains in the distance, and some huts in a circle, palm trees, a fire etc.,

On stage there is a raised throne, centre downstage. Maidens, warriors, children etc., of the tribe, are busying themselves about

Enter Warriors with Mrs Crusoe and Robinson

Warrior 1 You wait here. You prisoners of DONO-WYAR-SKIN tribe. *(exit)*
Robinson I wonder why it's called that?
Mrs Crusoe I DONO-WHY-ASKIN! *(I don't know, why you asking)* Oh I say! I am a one!
Robinson Mother! Be serious!

Enter Warriors with Rosie and Cedric

Warrior 1 You wait here. You prisoners of DONO-WYAR-SKIN tribe. *(exit)*
Cedric I say! I wonder why it's called that?
Mrs Crusoe *(encouraging the audience to join her)* I don't know. Why you asking?

Warriors enter with Captain and Mate

Warrior 1 You wait here. You prisoners of DONO-WYAR-SKIN tribe. *(exit)*
Mrs Crusoe *(to audience)* You ready?
Audience Yes.
Captain Batter me bilges! I wonder why it's called that?
Mrs Crusoe and **audience** I don't know. Why you asking?

Mrs Crusoe laughs loudly, enjoying her joke enormously

Enter Warriors with Man Friday. Mrs Crusoe is getting excited at the chance to say it again

Warrior 1 You wait here. You prisoner of DONO-WYAR-SKIN tribe.
Mrs Crusoe *(to audience)* Get ready!

The warriors exit. Mrs Crusoe looks at Man Friday expectantly. Man Friday looks around scared

Man Friday Help!
Mrs Crusoe Help? Is that all? Don't you want to know why they're called that?
Man Friday What?
Mrs Crusoe Why are they called that!
Man Friday I don't know. Why you asking? Ha, ha!
Mrs Crusoe You rotten spoilsport!

The warriors return and stands guard over the prisoners

Warrior 1 You be silent woman.
Mrs Crusoe Don't you 'woman' me! I demand to see the manager!
Warrior 1 You give manager indigestion.
Robinson Mother! Don't get yourself in a stew!
Mrs Crusoe I'm trying not to! That is a very tactless thing to say!
Cedric I say! What do you think's going on?
Man Friday We've been invited for dinner.
Cedric I hope it's not formal. I haven't got the old black tie what's it with me.
Rosie Shall we tell them we're not hungry?
Robinson I don't think they'd listen.
Rosie Robinson, I'm scared.
Robinson (*looking round for a way of escape*) We've got to try and escape Rosie.

Sound of drums again

Mrs Crusoe Oh good. It's the floor show starting!
Warrior 1 Make way for Big Chief Rumble Tum!

All bow as Chief Rumble Tum is carried on, and majestically takes his place on his throne

Mrs Crusoe Oh look! It's Terry Wogan!

Chief Rumble Tum claps his hands to signal that the dance should commence

Music No 13

Dance of the tribe's warriors and/or maidens. Complete with masks and spears, and to a suitable piece of music, they dance in front of the chief,

At the end of the dance

Mrs Crusoe I wonder why they're getting themselves all worked up?

Man Friday They need big appetite.

Mrs Crusoe It'll never get into the charts? I prefer a nice slow foxtrot myself.

Warrior 1 You be quiet woman. Talk is forbidden.

Captain Talk is forbidden! I'd like to see them keep 'er quiet!

Mrs Crusoe (*poking Warrior*) And don't you 'woman' me! I want to speak to the British Consul.

Warrior 1 You too late.

Mrs Crusoe Why?

Warrior 1 British Consul come to dinner last week.

Mrs Crusoe And?

Warrior 1 Delicious!

Mrs Crusoe Oh!

Rumble Tum Don't chat amongst yourselves. Bring the prisoners forward.

Warriors push them forward in front of throne

Warrior 1 Go!

Captain (*coming forward to speak up for himself*) Now hold 'ard, your corpulence! You and me is men o' the world. We can do a deal 'ere.

Rumble Tum You shut up.

Captain Now, now, your worshipfulness, I be a free man, a citizen of his majesty the king, ain't that right Polly?

Rumble Tum If you speak again we cut your Polly right off!

Cedric Look here old Rumble Jumble Sale what's it. We don't mean any harm.

Rumble Tum What you got for me to cut off eh?

Cedric Oh I say! Steady on old chap.

Rumble Tum What you all doin' on my island eh?

Mrs Crusoe Trying to get off!

Rumble Tum You too late! (*a distinctive laugh*) Ha, ha, ha!

Mrs Crusoe Here! Wait a minute! I'd know that silly laugh anywhere.

She pushes past the warriors and approaches the throne, taking a close look at Rumble Tum

Warrior 1 Not allowed approach Chief!

Mrs Crusoe Shut your face. I'll give him Rumble Tum! I was right. It is you Bert Crusoe!

They all look at each other in astonished disbelief

Rosie I don't believe it!

Robinson FATHER?

Mate Well, I'll be...

Rumble Tum Get her off me. She put evil eye on me!

Mrs Crusoe Where are they then?

Rumble Tum Where what?

A crash as she hits him. Everyone is astonished at her behaviour

Mrs Crusoe The frozen peas you fool! Thought you could hide eh? I'll give you frozen peas!

Rumble Tum (*completely changing character now*) Now wait a minute dear. I can explain everything.

Mrs Crusoe (*getting ready to murder him*) Don't you 'dear' me Bert Crusoe! You've got about ten seconds before I become a widow!

Rumble Tum/Bert Crusoe Well I was on my way to get the frozen peas you see.

Mrs Crusoe Yes? Well?

Bert Crusoe When I was abducted.

Mrs Crusoe Abducted! Huh! A likely story. Who'd want to abduct you? You'll have to do better than that!

Bert Crusoe It's true. Then I was taken to sea...

Mrs Crusoe To see what?

Bert Crusoe To sea, you see.

Mrs Crusoe I see, to sea eh?

Bert Crusoe Yes. In a ship. I was made to work hard for a couple of ship's biscuits a day.

Mrs Crusoe Go on. You've got a couple more seconds left on the clock.

Bert Crusoe When I got near this island I jumped overboard and swam ashore. The people here took me in.

Mrs Crusoe Like you're trying to take us all in, you mean?

Bert Crusoe No dear! They thought I must be some sort of god when I showed them my magnetic compass you see.

Mrs Crusoe You! Some sort of god! Pull the other one Bert Crusoe. I don't believe a word of it!

Bert Crusoe Every word is true dear. A nasty vicious sea captain took me. He had a parrot on his back, like him, that he was always talking to...

They all look round to see the Captain trying to sneak away

Wait a minute! That's him! (*signals to his warriors to bring the Captain forward*) Bring him here! Why you miserable...

Captain Now steady me old mess-mate, steady! It's not easy gettin' crews these days. I put's a notice up every week in the local job centre, but it's no good, you see. Ain't that right eh Polly?

Bert Crusoe I'll have to think of a special punishment for you.

Mrs Crusoe You won't have time for that.

Bert Crusoe Why's that dear?

Mrs Crusoe (*taking his ear*) Because you're coming straight home with me.

Bert Crusoe Yes dear. (*to the audience, as he goes*) All good things must come to an end! (*pointing to the ear that Mrs Crusoe is pulling*) EAR we go!

She exits with Bert Crusoe

Robinson Now you people keep an eye on the Captain here until we all get clear over the horizon. Then you can set him afloat in a barrel, with a couple of ladles for oars, and a ship's biscuit for supper.

General chorus of 'Yes' and 'Hurray'

Captain In a barrel! But that's undignified! (*slyly to Robinson*) Leave a drop o' rum in the barrel, for old time's sake. It's for old Polly's war wound, you see.

Robinson Who's laughing now Captain?

Captain Tarnish me telescope! It's enough to make a man turn honest! Ain't that... Oh shut your face!

Robinson Take him away.

Warriors take the Captain off, and return

Robinson (*to Rosie*) It's been quite an adventure, but now it's time to go home.

Rosie Yes. Time to go home, Robinson.

Song No 14 AUDIENCE SONG

A full chorus number, led by the principals they sing. 'Look for the Silver Lining' or 'Everything's Coming up Roses' or 'On a Wonderful Day Like Today'. This could, if preferred, be a short reprise of Song No 9

At the end of the song

Robinson Don't forget the treasure on the beach.

Cedric We won't forget that. Man Friday and I will take care of that for you.

Man Friday Yep positive.

Cedric And we'll let the Mate here help us. He's not a bad sort really.

Mate Thank you very much sir.

Rosie Then it's back to Plymouth, for the wedding of the year.

All shout 'Hurray'

Robinson I can't wait to see your mother's face when she finds out we're rich!

Rosie Nor can I! Everyone's invited to the wedding!

They all exit laughing. Curtain

Scene 4

An interact scene as the stage is set for the finale. This can be played in front of tabs, or a frontcloth showing the timbered interior of a Georgian house. Enter Mrs Crusoe, elegantly dressed

Mrs Crusoe Well here we are all home safe and sound. Robinson and Rosie are getting married. They've shared out the treasure so everyone is rich. I've just got one last thing to do, and then the wedding can get started. Can you guess what it is? Here she comes now, old Bossy-bloomers.

Enter Baroness Bossalot, now looking rather down at heel

Bossalot Ah there you are Mrs Crusoe. How nice to see you back home safe and sound.

Mrs Crusoe (*to the audience*) She won't think so in a minute. I'll bet that dress has a <u>long</u> interesting history!

Bossalot I just wanted to say that I hope our little differences can be forgotten now that you're, er, how shall I put it?

Mrs Crusoe Try stinking rich!

Bossalot Yes. Quite. Of course, I never had any real objections to my Rosie marrying your, er, Cuthbertson...

Mrs Crusoe Robinson, you silly old...

Bossalot Robinson, of course. It's just that one has to be so careful of what one's neighbours say, doesn't one?

Mrs Crusoe Oh one does, doesn't one!

Bossalot So glad you understand.

Mrs Crusoe I hear you've not been doing too well lately.

Bossalot No. I can't understand it. Some of my ships have gone astray. So tiresome! Investments, money all tied up you know. I've got a liquidity problem.

Mrs Crusoe You're pouring out of that dress alright.

Bossalot My assets have been frozen.

Mrs Crusoe You shouldn't sit on the freezer.

Bossalot My Times Index is falling.

Mrs Crusoe Dear, dear! Yes, I can see your stock market is sagging a bit! Or is it that dress? What a pity. I wonder how that could have happened? Queen Neptune seems not to have been smiling on you!

Bossalot What? What's Queen Neptune got to do with it?

Mrs Crusoe Oh nothing. I hear your castle up on the hill is for sale.

Bossalot Yes. It's too expensive to keep up, now that times have changed. Something smaller will suit me fine.

Mrs Crusoe Good. I'll buy you a dog kennel!

Bossalot What?

Mrs Crusoe You can have my old place if you like. I don't need it any more. We're moving up in the world.

Bossalot Really! Where?

Mrs Crusoe Up to your castle. I've just bought it!

Bossalot Oh no!

Mrs Crusoe Don't worry. I'll let you come and do a bit of cleaning, when you need the pocket money. To the wedding folks!

They both exit. The curtains open

Scene 5

Finale. Backcloth should show the Grand Reception Hall of a castle with; banners, armoury, bunting, a grand stairway, heraldic devices etc., Or, this could be the same set as for the opening scene, Plymouth Harbour. Everything is prepared for the wedding of Robinson Crusoe to Rosie, and the guests are arriving

Curtains open, there is a peel of church bells, and the Finale music begins

Song No 15

'Say, Robinson Crusoe, You're Really a Swell' to the tune of 'Gee, Officer Krupke' (West Side Story) or another. Any up-tempo number from the show would suit here. If the former is chosen, suggested words are;

> Say, Robinson Crusoe, you're really a swell.
> You found your long lost father, and some treasure as well.

So, Robinson Crusoe, if Rosie agrees.
You can get married when you please!

So naughty Captain Silver, is floating in a tub.
And dear old Mrs Crusoe, has found her long lost hub'
Now everyone is happy, And that cannot be bad.
Even Polly Parrot says he's glad!

We're sorry to tell you, it's time now to go.
To draw the final curtain, and to wind up the show.
We hope you enjoyed every moment of cheer.
See you again this time next year!

Cast now clap to the rhythm, as they sing this final chorus slowly

Say, Robinson Crusoe, you're really a swell.
You found your long lost father, and some treasure as well.
So, Robinson Crusoe, now Rosie agrees.
You can get married when you please.

Junior chorus; sea creatures, Neptune's assistants, warriors and maidens etc., enter and take their bows. They are followed by the adult chorus of; townsfolk, sailors, pirates, island natives etc., who take their bows

Principals now enter for walk down, in the following order

Olly
Warriors
Rumble Tum
Bossalot and **Queen Neptune**
Man Friday and **Cedric**
Captain and **Mate**
Mrs Crusoe

*There is now a loud cheer as **Rosie** and **Robinson** enter and take their bows*

Final chorus

Curtain

FURNITURE AND PROPERTY LIST

ACT 1

Scene 1

On stage: Barrels, boxes

Scene 2

Personal: Assorted luggage, and sock for **Mrs Crusoe**

Scene 3

On stage: Case, or platform for **Captain**
Off stage: Frying pan with egg for **Cedric**
Personal: Gun for **Captain**
               Labelled bottle for **Mrs Crusoe**
               Rope for **Mate**
               Sword for **Robinson**
               Daggers and guns for **Chorus**
               Cutlass for **Captain**

Scene 4

Personal: Clipboard for **Queen Neptune**
               Headdress for **Mate**
               Fisherman's hat, wellies, fishing net for **Cedric**
               Umbrella, flippers, snorkel mask, mack for **Mrs Crusoe**

Scene 5

On stage: Throne, tin of Whiskas, wreckage etc.,
Off stage: Song word board, if required

ACT 2

Scene 1

On stage: Seat for **Mrs Crusoe** and **Captain**, tools for **Man Friday**
Personal: Football scarf for **Man Friday**
               Shovel for **Mate**

Sock for **Mrs Crusoe**
Mixing bowl and spoon for **Mrs Crusoe**
Coins for **Robinson**
Gun for **Captain**

Scene 3

On stage: Throne

LIGHTING PLOT

ACT 1
Scene 1

Open:	Bright 'Sunny Day' exterior lighting	Page 1
Cue 1	As **Mrs Crusoe** goes down into the audience	Page 3
	House lights up. Cut as she comes back on stage	
Cue 2	As curtains close	Page 10
	Blackout	

Scene 2

Open:	General exterior lighting	Page 10

Scene 3

Open:	Bright sunny exterior lighting	Page 12
Cue 3	*Lights up and down as thunder rolls*	Page 19
	and lightning flashes. Gradually dim	
	lighting through to end of scene	
Cue 4	*Lightning flashes more intense. General*	Page 20
	lighting down to dim as thunder becomes louder	
Cue 5	*Lights slowly out as curtains close*	Page 20

Scene 4

Open:	Moderate general lighting. Green filter	Page 20

Scene 5

ACT 2

Scene 1

Scene 2

Scene 3

Scene 4

Scene 5

EFFECTS PLOT

General suggestions are given. The amount, and complexity, of effects will depend on the director, the size, and type, of orchestra. Where I have suggested thunder rolls, this can be achieved by; cymbals crashing, a percussion drum roll, or dramatic chords on the piano. Or you may wish to use special, back stage effects for these noises.

A few chords on the piano should suffice as "entry music", if needed. A few notes of a hornpipe for the Captain, for instance.

ACT 1	*Cue 1*	As **Mrs Crusoe** paces up and down *Agitated cymbals*	Page 2
	Cue 2	As **Mate** is kicked by **Captain** *Crash*	Page 8
	Cue 3	As **Mrs Crusoe** paces about again *Agitated cymbals*	Page 12
	Cue 4	As **Captain's** gun is fired *Loud bang*	Page 12
	Cue 5	As **Mate** drinks *Background playing of 'What shall* *we do with the drunken sailor'*	Page 17
	Cue 6	As lights flash *Continuous thunder rolls*	Page 19
	Cue 7	As lights flash brighter *Louder thunder sounds*	Page 20
	Cue 8	As **Queen Neptune** enters *Distant thunder rolls*	Page 20
	Cue 9	As **Captain** hits **Mate** *Crash*	Page 25
	Cue 10	As **Mate** turns to see Olly *Crash*	Page 26
	Cue 11	As **Captain** sees Olly *Crash*	Page 27
ACT 2	*Cue 12*	As **Captain** hits **Mate** *Crash*	Page 32
	Cue 13	At **Mate** 'Nobody's going to look there' *Background music 'Dambusters' up* *Fade at **Captain** 'Here she comes now'*	Page 33
	Cue 14	At **Mrs Crusoe** 'All of a doo daa' *Music 'There's no place like home' up.* *Fade at **Captain** 'Bakin' in oven'*	Page 34
	Cue 15	As **Captain** struggles to get shoes off **Mrs Crusoe** *Bangs and crashes*	Page 35
	Cue 16	**Mrs Crusoe** empties bowl on **Captain** *Crash*	Page 35
	Cue 17	As **Captain** hits **Mate** *Crashes*	Page 35

PRODUCTION NOTES

Scenery

The period here, unlike many pantomimes, is Georgian. Most of the scenery is straightforward. The script contains detailed notes at the beginning of each scene. Each major scene is interspaced with an interact scene, to be played in front of tabs, or a frontcloth, while the main scenes are set up. This allows a continuous performance through each act.

Ship Scene can be effectively decked out with rigging, barrels, boxes, flags, and as much paraphernalia as your props can summon up, and your stage take, and still leave room for dancing!

Underwater Scene should be as different and unusual as possible, with as much use of lighting effects, yellows, greens and blues, and possibly strange sounds as well, to make this a spectacular finish to the first half. You can afford to place a collection of effective properties; anchors, ship's wheels etc., on here, since there is plenty of time to re-set during the interval.

Beach Scene can have a wigwam-type tent on stage, or painted into the backcloth. A tripod, unlit, fire possibly, so long as it is clear of the dancers.

Finale Scene may be a new set, or, it could be the harbour scene again.

Songs and Dances

Fifteen musical numbers are included here. Each should last about two minutes. Don't let them go on too long. Remember the golden rule - leave your audience wanting more. You may not wish to use the numbers I have suggested. Some groups may want to use more. Keep the dances as different as possible. and vary the suggestions given according to your own strengths.

Costumes

The costumes should suggest the "Georgian" period, although many pantomime characters, the Dame for instance, have established traditional 'medieval pantomime' type costumes, that are expected by the audience.

Baroness Bossalot will be richly dressed in the opening scene, to contrast with a 'down at heel' costume at the end. **Robinson** will wear a short tunic, tights, soft boots, belt and hat, in warm, interesting colours. One costume will suffice, except for the walk down when he should be upgraded. **Rosie** also will only need to change for walk down. A simple dress, or skirt and 'Snow White' type blouse and waistcoat is suggested. **Mrs Crusoe** will, of course be 'over the top', with a number of outrageous costumes. the usual armoury of; gaudy jewellery, makeup, colourful bloomers, incredible hats etc., should be included here. **Captain** may wear a dishevelled captain's uniform, that has seen better days. As a completely eccentric character, you can 'go to town' and fit him with, admiral's hat, gold braid, row of unlikely medals etc., The most important feature of his costume is, of course, the parrot. Some ingenuity is called for to make this effective. It can be made of papier mache, cloth and feathers etc., It must be securely fixed, since the Captain is active. Possibly a framework, or shaped rod, fitted under the costume. How elaborate you want to be with the operation of the parrot will depend on the ingenuity of the actor and props. He could have a turning head, opening mouth, closing eyes, all operated by a dexterous performer, given the right apparatus. The **Mate**, and the rest of the crew, can be dressed as a mixture of pirates and sailors, with striped shirts, bright head scarves, eye patches, dark trousers and shoes, with daggers, guns, knives etc., at their belts. **Cedric** is a toff, with maybe a distinctive top hat, monocle, bow tie, to suit his character. **Queen Neptune** (who can double up with Baroness Bossalot) should be regally dressed, in a full-length costume and tiara. She is a 'fairy godmother' type to Robinson and Rosie, so the costume can suggest such a character. **Man Friday, Rumble Tum,** and **Islanders** will wear ragged or grass skirts, painted faces, shirts and blouses, all the same, or a range of colours. **Rumble Tum** can have a crown, or large hat, to set him aside from the rest. Possibly with a bowler, or umbrella, saved from his previous existence as Bert Crusoe. **Man Friday** has a football scarf. **Warriors** to carry spears. **Olly** a specially made costume of grey, with lots of arms. He could be Sammy the Starfish, Lennie the Lobster. Whatever you prefer to costume.

I wish you great fun with this pantomime.

Jim Sperinck